Worki

Working as One

Fundamental Conversations
That Build Cooperation & Get Results

Christine C. Williams, PhD

Working as One

Manufactured in the United States of America

For information, please contact:
Brown Books Publishing Group
16200 North Dallas Parkway, Suite 170
Dallas, Texas 75248
www.brownbooks.com
972-381-0009
A New Era in Publishing™

ISBN-13: 978-1-933285-95-5
ISBN-10: 1-933285-95-8
LCCN 2007932705
1 2 3 4 5 6 7 8 9 10

To my teachers

Table of Contents

Thank You

Acknowledgments

I am most grateful to the many people who have influenced my thinking and work as a facilitator. Not only have you helped instill in me a lifelong passion for working with others to support healthy conversations, but you have also taught me to value and honor the integrity, authenticity, and presence required during these interactions.

I wish to acknowledge the many clients I have been privileged to work with. You have taught me so much and have enriched my life beyond measure. I would especially like to thank my many colleagues and friends at the Department of Veterans Affairs, Veterans Health Administration. Your professionalism and dedication to quality patient care have made the VA the excellent health care system it is today. I'm proud to have been a small part of your efforts.

I could not have written this book without the support of my friends and family, including my mom, dad, sister, and brother. To my dad in particular—your enthusiastic words after reading my manuscript gave me enough encouragement to last a lifetime. I came to discover that the initial writing was the easy part. The follow-through actions were far more challenging. To those who continued to encourage me—thanks. I took your advice and stuck with it.

I am deeply indebted to my first reader, Jeanne Berry, who spent hours working with me following my first draft. Your encouraging words and sound advice kept me going. To Susan Larson— thank you for your first edit, as well as for helping me to connect with the wonderful team at Brown Books Publishing. I also wish to thank my peer reviewers: Judy James, Sue Klein, Joan Leppla, Stephanie Woods, and Chuck Rankin. Sharing your perspectives were acts of friendship that went above and beyond, and I am appreciative of your suggestions and support.

Most of all, to my husband Joe—thanks for your continual love and support and for being a part of my journey.

Introduction

Getting Straight to the Point: What's This Book About?

Like it or not, if you want to get things done in your workplace, you have to talk and reach agreements with others. Talking isn't always convenient or easy, but it's an essential tool for building cooperation and getting results.

Working as One gives you a framework of seven fundamental conversations, four guiding principles to support you in your conversations, and specific tools to talk and reach agreements with your co-workers. Using this framework, you'll find yourself more able to talk about the right things in the right way—with increased skill and confidence. You'll also find that you and your co-workers are more focused on what's really important and in sync with how and when the work gets done.

As a facilitator of workplace conversations for many years, I've witnessed frustration, anger, confusion, and divisiveness among some co-workers. I've also seen enthusiasm, pride, and cohesiveness among others. As a result, I am continually driven to ask the questions, "What's the difference? Despite the physical environment, amount of work, or personalities, why do some people work well together while others are continually at odds with one another?"

One of the major differences is that people who work well together talk regularly with one another about matters of mutual importance. They engage in fundamental conversations, those conversations so central to the functioning of a group that it is difficult for the group to conduct their work without them. The conversations can be interpersonal or task-related in nature. The agreements reached among co-workers as a result of the conversations are not sporadic; rather, they are a natural way of conducting business—all the time.

Working as One is based on three premises:

- The very nature of our work necessitates that we function as part of an interdependent system rather than as separate individuals.

- To work together, we need to talk with one another in productive and constructive ways. There are fundamental conversations that help us recognize, foster, and honor a systems approach to our work.

- When co-workers think and act in ways that develop and support their capacities to conduct and honor fundamental conversations, they create a more focused, collaborative, and meaningful way of life in the workplace.

● WHO SHOULD READ THIS BOOK?

Working as One is intended for anyone who has to work with others to get things accomplished. In the context of this book, **workplace** is defined as any place where people come together for some intended purpose or effort, either on a paid or volunteer basis. **Co-workers** are defined as anyone who works with others to provide a product, service, or outcome, either on a paid or volunteer basis.

The type or configuration of the workplace and co-workers may vary, and there could be two or two hundred people involved in the conversation. Examples include workgroups in hospitals, schools, businesses, or government; boards of directors or committees for non-profit organizations; community athletic programs; and so forth. The common denominator is that the people are connected in some way to provide a product, service, or outcome and that, to properly conduct their work, they have to talk and reach agreements with one another about fundamental issues.

The book is divided into three major sections with each section corresponding to a major question related to fundamental conversations in the workplace:

Part I responds to the question, *"Why do we need to talk with one another?"* It explores the nature of our work in today's world and provides a context and rationale for the importance of working together. **Part II** responds to the question, *"What do we need to talk about?"* Seven fundamental conversations are described, each having specific trigger questions that serve to stimulate and focus co-workers' discussions. **Part III** responds to the question, *"How do we go about having these conversations?"* This section provides an overall framework and method to conduct and honor fundamental conversations. Included is a description of a "conversation cycle" and four suggested guidelines that support and enrich the use of that cycle. Also included are several toolkit questions and phrases to help co-workers demonstrate effective communication skills.

As you will discover, there's nothing fancy about fundamental conversations. All you need is a fair amount of common sense and a great deal of commitment and persistence. It doesn't require external sources (such as organizational development gurus, consultants, or facilitators, etc.) to provide answers, although these sources can be helpful in providing expertise, guidance, and direction. Mostly, the conversations call for you and your co-workers to think for yourselves (perhaps very differently than before) and accept responsibility for who you are, what you're about, and how you choose to do business with each other and your customers.

Why Do We Need to Talk With One Another?

● WORKING AS ONE

For most of us, the nature of our work necessitates that we function as part of an interdependent system rather than as separate individuals. Whether we volunteer for a community Block Watch program, work for a film production company, or serve as the CEO for a major corporation, we *need* other people to get things done. In our jobs, homes, communities, and volunteer organizations, we experience situations where working together as a cohesive unit creates better overall results. Success requires a group effort with each individual contributing a critical piece to the overall task at hand.

Like the human body, all parts have a purpose. To function properly, each part must do its job *in relation to the whole*. Imagine trying to walk down the street with one part of our body trying to "do its own thing" without the other parts. You wouldn't get very far, very fast. Yet that is often what happens when we work with others, whether it's intentional or not. We take our part of the work and move forward, often without awareness or consideration of how our thoughts and behaviors impact others' efforts. As a result, the work becomes disjointed. To do even the simplest tasks requires increasingly more energy.

This disjointed approach happens in our personal, as well as our work, relationships. Many years ago my husband Joe and I had a little powerboat. We were boating in a nearby lake one day when a summer storm began to brew. Our engine died in a marshy area about fifty yards from shore. After repeated tries to get the motor started, we decided to row to the boat ramp using the oars we kept for emergencies.

What started out as a fairly simple task (use the oars to row to a specific destination) soon turned into a nightmare! As the sky darkened, each of us went to opposite sides of the boat. Completely ignoring each other, Joe rowed in one direction while I rowed in another. All we did was move in circles. The storm was approaching quickly, and there didn't seem to be time to stop and talk. We started to bark orders at one another, each believing we had the "correct" answer. After a bit more shouting and name-calling, we finally worked out a system that got us close enough for Joe to hop out of the boat and drag us to the ramp.

By that time the two of us were barely speaking. We had made it to the shore but at what cost?

I learned two valuable lessons that day. First, it's important to take the time (as little as a minute would have sufficed in the boating incident) to talk things through and reach some basic agreements rather than independently proceeding with the task at hand. Without each other's cooperation we simply couldn't move forward. Second, I recognized how much our words and actions influence the speed and stress level of accomplishing an outcome, as well as our ongoing relationship with each other.

Over the years, as my experience as a group facilitator grew, I saw similar situations repeated and magnified in organizational settings all over the country. Just as in the boating incident, there was lots of spinning in circles; one person not knowing or caring what another person was doing, people expending energy on words and tasks that were relatively unimportant in the scheme of the overall work, increasing anger and frustration about the unnecessary confusion, and on and on.

● WHAT IS IT YOU WANT?

"What is it you want?" I ask of groups, as I work to help them clarify their workplace issues and concerns. "In the end, after this specific conversation, what outcomes do you want to achieve?"

The answers vary, but beyond the rhetoric and buzzwords, a common theme emerges. As a woman in one group so aptly stated, "We want to work better together." "Well, what does that mean?" I ask. And the answers go something like this:

- We want to accomplish the work of this organization (group, etc.) in a way that satisfies our customers (clients, those we serve) without going crazy doing it.

- We want to come to work (paid or volunteer) knowing why we're here, what our job requires, and how it connects with the work of others.

- We want to know the "rules" unique to our organization and have a common understanding of what a job well done really means, how decisions are made, how resources are distributed, and what behaviors and actions get rewarded.

- We want everyone to play by these rules, for all of us to walk the talk.

- We want to know what the work priorities are and where we should spend our time and energy.

- We want people to treat one another with decency, respect, and common consideration.

- We want to be heard, have our opinions valued, and have our knowledge and expertise appreciated.

If anything is surprising here, it is that these responses are so simple. There's nothing extraordinary about them. As a respected health care executive once told me, "This isn't rocket science. Most people just want the basics to do their work."

What I *do* find extraordinary is that people who work together don't often talk about these important matters. In fact, some people go to great lengths not to talk with one another. I frequently ask groups to tell me when they last spoke about these issues with one another. Most often the response is "never." In other cases, they had been discussed ad nauseam but with no follow through or connection to the work. It's a workplace reality. We wonder why we continue to spin in our workplace boats when we have yet to discuss, agree, and act upon the most fundamental workplace issues.

● BUT WHAT IF . . . ?

What if people who worked together had productive and relevant conversations about fundamental issues that affected the essence of their work? What if agreements were made (based upon these conversations) that were honored and improved upon on an ongoing basis? What if co-workers not only talked about the issues, but also integrated their agreements into the day-to-day functioning, decision-making, and resource allocation within the organization? And finally, what if they shared their agreements and findings with others outside their immediate workgroup who were part of a larger system that needed this information in order to appropriately interface with the group?

Imagine a workplace (job, volunteer, community) where you and your co-workers:

- Share an agreed-upon understanding about the end results you want to achieve collectively.

- Share an agreed-upon understanding of the purpose of your work.

- Are clear about the core values that drive the organization and influence co-workers' behaviors and decision-making on a daily basis.

- Recognize who the customers are and what they need to feel satisfied.

- Understand each other's roles, responsibilities, and authority and how each individual interfaces with others in order to accomplish the work.

- Share an understanding of the organizational plan and priorities, knowing where to focus work efforts and how to measure work progress and success.

- Have agreed-upon structures and processes to communicate, resolve conflict, make decisions, and demonstrate appreciation and support for one another.

Is this possible? I think so. Many of us have experienced the joy of working productively with a group of people to achieve common goals, both in and out of the traditional workplace. Yet those experiences seem to be the exception rather than the norm. In general, our workplace cultures are not yet at a stage that embraces and supports these practices on a regular basis.

● MOVING BEYOND THE BARRIERS

The biggest barrier we face in practicing an interdependent approach to our work is our own way of thinking. Many of us grew up in an era where we identified with and admired those who demonstrated individualistic thinking and behaviors. As we watched television and movies, we came to believe that the real heroes were the folks who, despite incredible odds, single-handedly overcame obstacles on the battlefield, athletic field, business field, or wherever. They appeared to be tough, decisive, strong-willed, and single-minded in their approach; and they certainly didn't need others' advice, knowledge, or expertise before taking action. They were invincible.

We can still have heroes, but it's an illusion to think their success is single-handed. In reality, the single-handed approach simply doesn't get the job done, not then or now. Imagine trying to run a community theatre, provide health care, educate children, or govern constituents in isolation from everyone else. To get a significant impact, we need significant support from others. Even though we may create something individually, we can't sustain it all by ourselves. We need a collective group effort.

Intellectually, we may understand this concept, but when it comes time to act in ways that focus on "we" rather than "me" behaviors in our work lives, we lose sight of our need to function as part of a larger system. Consider the manager who exceeds his budget without caring how his actions will impact other managers' budgets within his division; the worker who continually fails to meet project deadlines, causing chaos for co-workers who must work overtime to compensate for those delays; or the customer service representative who promises prompt delivery on a manufacturing part, only to learn that she was never informed of a decision made six months ago to discontinue the part's production.

Changing our mind-set and behaviors to incorporate a systems approach to our work is not as complex as it seems. I once went on a wagon train through the Teton Mountains. Bud and Ben (the draft horses who pulled our wagon) were able to demonstrate a simple systems approach. Bud couldn't go one way and Ben another without comical and potentially dangerous results. They had to be going in the same direction, each doing his job in harmony with the other in order for us to arrive at our destination without mishap or delay.

In our work lives, it's more difficult. Rarely are we in an environment that remains static and unchanged. Unlike Bud and Ben, we often don't know what the workplace terrain is going to look like from one moment to the next. You start out thinking your department has X amount of dollars and the budget is suddenly reduced by 50 percent. You think you've got one-hundred volunteers for the community "chicken fest," and only twenty people show up the night of the event. You think your company location is stable and then find out the corporate office is moving across the country.

Bud and Ben also didn't experience the quickening pace and personal stress that accompanies human work life. Often, the more work you do, the more you are given and the faster you are expected to finish. For example, in the classic *I Love Lucy* television show, Lucy and Ethel are working in the chocolate factory and have the job of wrapping individual pieces of candy moving along a conveyor belt. As the belt starts moving, all is well. They are able to pick up each piece of candy, wrap it, and place it back on the belt. But gradually the belt starts to move faster. Soon Lucy and Ethel are in a state of frenzy. They can't wrap the candy fast enough. They're stuffing the candy in their pockets, mouths, hats, and dresses just to try and keep up with the pace. It's an impossible task, and eventually the whole process breaks down!

As our workplace terrain continues to change and the pace becomes faster, the likelihood for breakdowns of communication and procedures increases. Just at the very time we need to address and honor our interdependence, knowing that we need each other to get things done, we often retreat into a self-centered, territorial, or protective mode. Unable to control the situation, people feel angry and victimized and blame one another.

What we really want to do is get everyone moving in the same direction (just like Bud and Ben) with a minimal amount of stress and pain. We need to view our work from a systems perspective (to see how each of our individual contributions affects the whole) and then determine collectively how to best work together to achieve our mutual goals. In order to make this happen, plain and simple, *we have to talk with one another!* Fundamental conversations get us talking about the right things.

● A FUNDAMENTAL CONVERSATION—WHAT IT IMPLIES

In the context of this book the word *conversation* implies three specific things.

- There is a purpose for the conversation with specific outcomes to be derived from it (this is not just talking to "shoot the breeze").

- The conversation allows for all parties to engage in both talking and listening. Everyone has equal rights to articulate their thoughts, listen actively, and ask questions.

- There are appropriate follow-through behaviors and actions that directly relate to any agreements made during the conversation.

● IMPLICATION #1:

A Purpose for the Conversation

The amount of time people spend in meetings where much is said but with little results has become a national workplace joke. Groups frequently come together with no agenda or stated meeting outcomes. For a fundamental conversation to be productive, the parties involved in the conversation should be able to articulate the meeting purpose and what they hope to walk away with by the end of their communication.

This is *not* to say that every conversation we engage in throughout the day should be productive or outcome-driven. Nor is it to say that every conversation has to result in an immediate answer or action. In the book *The Fifth Discipline Fieldbook*, Rick Ross builds on the work of Peter Senge, a leader in the area of creating organizations that value learning and use it as a constructive means to increase efficiency, productivity, and a sense of meaning in our workplaces. Ross describes a continuum of interactions that people frequently engage in as they talk with one another. These interactions are categorized into four major areas: raw debate, polite discussion, skillful discussion, and dialogue.

The interactions of raw debate and polite discussion lean toward the less productive forms of interaction. The intent in raw debate is to "win" while the polite discussion is a more relaxed form of interacting, which does not require the participants to take a stand or push their thought processes. Although raw debate is not encouraged since little gets accomplished in a verbal sparring match, polite discussion can make our days a lot more pleasant.

However, as we collectively conduct our work, it is the interactions of skillful discussion and dialogue that can help us the most. The primary difference between these two interactions is one of intention. In skillful discussion, the purpose is to problem-solve or bring some sort of closure—either to make a decision, reach an agreement, or develop plans that are followed by appropriate actions. When we refer to dialogue, the intent of the interaction is to provide opportunities for exploration, discovery, and insight.

The heart of fundamental conversations builds on the concept and practice of skillful discussion. The results are very concrete. The aim is for co-workers to reach agreements and, if that's not possible, to continue to explore those areas where disagreements still exist. Dialogue is also valuable, for it can expand a group's thinking to gain a deeper understanding of an issue or explore options that they might otherwise not have considered. Too often a group is so focused on a specific problem that they fail to see a larger, more systemic approach.

● IMPLICATION #2:
Allows for All Involved Parties to Engage in Both Talking and Listening

The second implication of a fundamental conversation is that people listen as well as talk. Everyone has equal rights and is encouraged to actively listen, ask questions, and articulate their thoughts.

When you actively listen, you allow time for the speaker to finish their sentences and express their thoughts, make eye contact with the person speaking, and rephrase (in your own words) to the speaker what you are hearing them say. Then you pause to check for accuracy. When you combine active listening with asking questions for further information and clarification, you build a bridge to shared meaning and understanding.

One of the biggest things to keep in mind when we converse with others, no matter what the circumstances, is that we carry a host of assumptions with us. We all do it, sometimes without even realizing it. We have assumptions about how others think or feel, what they mean when they make a particular statement, and why they behave a particular way.

We assume we understand what the other person is trying to say, but in fact, we may have no idea at all! The trick is not so much to stop doing it but to be aware of how much it influences our own perceptions and any interactions and decisions that follow.

Several years ago my father-in-law passed away at the age of eighty-seven. The family, all from out of town, gathered with my eighty-year-old mother-in-law to attend the funeral. My mother-in-law mentioned how grateful she was for the support of her church. She was particularly delighted that those cute "Smith" boys with their big smiles had brought a variety of cold cuts over to her house. I was pleased to hear how helpful the young people were at the church, knowing they'd be a continued source of comfort for her.

At the funeral home, an elderly gentleman approached me to offer his condolences and introduced himself as Ken, one of the Smith boys. Imagine my utter shock to discover that the Smith boys weren't teenagers, but grown men! Later, I spoke with my mother-in-law. "I thought you said those Smiths were *boys*. That man had to be in his seventies!" I exclaimed. She looked at me incredulously and responded, "Well, they're boys to *me!* We've known each other since we were kids. Everyone always referred to them as the Smith *boys,* and I guess the name just stuck. Aren't they sweet?"

Everyone had a good laugh, including the Smith *boys*. Clearly, my assumption of the term *boys* was not in the same context as my mother-in-law and the rest of her church community.

Although many inaccurate assumptions are relatively harmless, this story reminds us just how easily and frequently misunderstandings occur in our everyday lives.

For example, there is a classic article, by Jerry Harvey, later made into a training video, titled *The Abilene Paradox*. The setting is a small ranch in west Texas. A mother, father, daughter, and her husband are sitting on the front porch on a scorching Sunday afternoon trying to remain cool. Someone suggests going to Abilene for lunch, which is a good hour's drive away. There's a brief, not very enthusiastic discussion, but in the end, everyone says that "yes" that's what they'd like to do.

Three hours later, the family is again sitting on the front porch. They have just returned from Abilene. They're hot, dusty, tired, and cranky. The car had no air conditioning. Someone says something like they wish they hadn't gone into Abilene, in fact they never wanted to. They just did it to please the others. Pretty soon everyone is saying the same thing; that it was a terrible idea and *whose* idea was this anyway? Together, they reviewed their earlier discussion, noting who said what. They realized that although they had all verbalized their willingness to go, each person only did so because they assumed they understood what each of the other individuals meant. They collectively made the decision to spend a very uncomfortable afternoon in a hot car and stuffy restaurant, based on the false assumption that other family members really wanted to go to Abilene. A little more time spent talking, asking questions, and actively listening could have made a world of difference in their day.

On a more serious note, I once taught in an inner city high school where as a homeroom teacher I was expected to collect a parental excuse for an absence within three days of the student's return to school. Without it, the student would serve detention. One day I asked a student if she had her parental excuse. Janet, knowing the rules and not being too happy about them, told me and the rest of the class what I could do with "my" excuse. When the bell rang for the first class period I asked her to stay to talk privately, but she refused so I sent her to the principal's office.

Later that day Janet came to talk with me, by way of a wise assistant principal. We had a good conversation. We took time to express ourselves, listen, and ask questions of each other. I learned that the previous night her parents had gotten into a violent argument, ending with her mother shooting her father and her father knifing her mother. No one was fatally injured, but needless to say, Janet was traumatized by the event. The fact that she even came to school the next day was amazing. She assumed that no one at school was going to cut her a break or even care that this had happened. When I asked her for her excuse, she thought I was cold and uncaring. I assumed she was being a smart aleck. My perception of the situation and the required disciplinary actions was greatly altered by our conversation. Her assumptions about how the assistant principal and I felt about her also changed. What was particularly striking about this experience is that without the talking, listening, and asking questions we would have had no basis for shared understanding. Decisions would have been made based on inaccurate assumptions.

● **IMPLICATION #3:**

Appropriate Follow-through Behaviors and Actions

The third implication of the word conversation, as used in this book, pertains to appropriate follow-through behaviors and actions that directly relate to honoring agreements made during the conversation. In working with groups, I find this is an aspect that really hits home. Without the follow through, talking means nothing.

When you engage in fundamental conversations, agreements are reached that influence the work of the group. However, the actions you take when you walk out the door are what bring those words to life. The actions align what you say with what you do.

Many groups engage in very powerful fundamental conversations, yet weeks or months later they are angry and frustrated because nothing has changed. For fundamental conversations to be relevant, people must follow through with concrete behaviors and actions that are consistent with their agreements. This includes changing individual and collective behaviors as well as the appropriate redistribution of resources such as time, money, or energy. Monitoring these behaviors and resources on a regular basis to capture lessons learned and allow for further adjustments and improvements of the agreements is also critical.

Part Two

What Do We Need to Talk About?

● **SEVEN FUNDAMENTAL CONVERSATIONS**

There are seven fundamental conversations every group of people working together should engage in at some time. These conversations are intended to help groups focus their efforts in a common direction in a manner that is efficient and productive with a minimal amount of stress. Each conversation area has several trigger questions. These trigger questions are designed to stimulate group discussion about the specific conversation area. Groups may select one or all of these trigger questions or create their own.

The overall outcome for each conversation (what you want to walk away with at the end of the discussion) is a *shared* understanding of *individual* perspectives and a *collective* understanding of *group* agreements as they relate to the trigger question(s).

This requires a monumental shift in thinking from "me" (what do I want?) to "we" (what do we collectively agree on?). The *collective* understanding and agreements (followed by consistent actions and behaviors) are what gets people moving in the same direction.

● **CONVERSATION #1:**

VISION

Trigger Questions:

- What's the end result we're trying to create?

- What do we want to be known for?

- What are we striving to achieve?

When you talk about *vision*, you're trying to gain a shared understanding of the product, service, or outcome you want to create. In his book *The Seven Habits of Highly Effective People*, Stephen Covey refers to it as "beginning with the end in mind."

Creating and sharing visions is one of those timeless conversations. From our earliest beginnings, people who have lived and worked together talked about their dreams for the future. Thinking of some of the world's great creations—the United States Constitution, the pyramids of Egypt, the Taj Mahal—we can see how groups, working together with a strong vision, can accomplish remarkable things. These visions, if strong enough, can be sustained for hundreds, if not thousands, of years.

While on a trip in India, I was fortunate to visit the caves at Ajanta and Ellora, northeast of Bombay. These extraordinary caves were built by Buddhist, Hindu, and Jain monks and other artisans over a period of several hundred years. The caves display some of the finest stonework and paintings ever created. They are an architectural wonder in that they were built from the top down out of a huge rock face on the side of a hill using only simple tools. Initially, an outline was made on the rock face. Then the excavators moved in and worked downwards from the top so that the ceiling was completed first. The carving had to be mistake-proof, for once the stone was cut it could not be replaced. As each patch was cleared, the painters, sculptors, and finishers began their work.

This is a remarkable example of the power of vision in action. Just think about it. Some Buddhist monks got together at Ajanta three hundred years B.C. and shared a vision for creating a place of beauty and harmony that they were able to sustain for eight hundred years. A monk working in one century could have been finishing work on a painting begun one hundred years earlier. The original painter was long gone and yet the current monk had a clear enough sense of the original, and probably expanded vision, to complete the effort. What an incredible accomplishment!

Our work lives are rarely that dramatic. But without a *shared* vision, there's no impetus to move forward as a cohesive group. All you have is a bunch of people with their own mini-visions moving in different directions, all the while bumping into one another. Without vision, chaos and confusion become the organizational norm.

For example, there was a group of dedicated people representing various educational institutions within a geographic area. They had been asked by a state agency to work together to improve the use of technology in their classrooms. Major funding dollars were available if the group could come up with a workable plan. The effort was intended to be collaborative, with the resource dollars being used for equipment, training, or projects that could potentially benefit all of the institutions. After nearly a year of monthly meetings, the group felt they really had nothing to show for their efforts. They had exchanged information and made a few decisions, but as a group, they were disconnected and lacked focus.

The group was struggling because they had never reached a shared understanding of what they were trying to create. They had never clearly articulated their thoughts with one another about what "improved use of technology" really meant. Group members had been operating on sets of individual assumptions that had in no way been agreed upon by the group as a whole.

In simple terms, they had yet to ask and agree upon what they really wanted to see happen with these funding dollars. They were heading down a path with no clear destination.

I was asked to work with the group to help them focus. Our first step was to create a shared vision. Visions don't have to be fancy or complicated to be meaningful. In most cases, a vision statement should be brief with a few sentences or phrases that are easily understood.

Once the group actually concentrated their discussion on the question, "What is it we really want to see happen?" the transformation was immediate. They were able to share individual perspectives and reach a collective agreement about their vision within a couple of hours. Their co-created vision statement read, "For the region to have an educational system where technology is integrated throughout the learning process."

Once the vision statement was created and understood, the group was able to move right into developing their mission statement (what their group actually does to create the vision) followed by the identification of their goals for the next year. One year later, the group felt that, not only had their vision statement been the guiding beacon for their planning efforts and implementation accomplishments, it remained relevant for their future efforts as well.

The creation of vision statements has become quite popular in recent years. In the lobby of many businesses, educational institutions, or corporations they can be found displayed on the walls for all to see. Even though the traditional working world at large has begun to pay attention to such an important facet of how to conduct business, this vision stuff isn't just for the big guys. You and I can incorporate "vision talk" as part of our everyday lives.

As the volunteer coach for the community soccer team for elementary children, I'd better be clear about the kind of program we're trying to create. Imagine if one coaching member thinks "winning is everything" and another coaching member thinks that "no matter what, every kid gets equal playing time, because we're trying to teach the importance of being a part of a team." Those are two very different visions. If a coaching staff (and community members) never put the issue on the table for discussion, it's hard to know which player behaviors to reinforce and which to discourage.

Similarly, if I work as a bus driver for a local school district, it helps to have a collective agreement and understanding about what we (as a group of bus drivers) are trying to create for the students who get on and off our buses every day. A vision statement as simple as, "We want to create a transportation system that provides a safe, caring, dependable service for our kids," can shape future actions and behaviors in terms of how all bus drivers do their jobs.

The power is not simply in the statement itself. The power is that a group of bus drivers (who know their business better than anyone else) sat down and hashed out their different perspectives about what they wanted to see as a bottom line for the kids (their customers) who ride their buses. The people engaged in the discussion have created a baseline for how they do their work. As a bus driver in this district, I now fully recognize that it's not only part of my job to provide a safe environment but I'm also expected to be caring and dependable. I understand what the words caring, safe, and dependable really mean in the context of my work. I realize that I am one member of a larger group and that it's not okay for me to "run my bus the way I please." All children, no matter what bus they are on, should have the same standard of safety, caring, and dependability.

● CONVERSATION #2:
MISSION

Trigger Questions:

- What is our collective purpose?

- Why do we exist?

- What do we do—what are our basic functions?

The word mission implies purpose. A mission statement should be a very concrete, down-to-earth statement that tells what a particular group actually does. By its very nature, a mission defines parameters and helps determine how a group spends its time, energy, and resources.

During the 1991 Gulf War, the United States military mission was to end the Iraqi presence in Kuwait, no more, no less. When the Iraqis departed from Kuwait, the war (as it had been defined) was officially over. The general public understood this clear, concise mission.

In the original *Mission Impossible* television series, each show began with the lead character getting his assignment: "Your mission, should you choose to accept it, is to . . ." A mission statement was a part of every directive Jim Phelps was given. Even the crew of *Star Trek* had a specific mission—to "seek out new life and new civilizations. To boldly go where no man has gone before."

People often get hung up and confused over the difference between mission and vision. Vision is the big picture of what your group is striving to accomplish (the end result). Mission relates to your group's particular job in making the vision happen. The mission helps direct what your group will actually *do*.

For example, President Kennedy painted a vision of travel in space, but he and Congress gave NASA the specific mission to deliver a man on the moon. In the movie *Apollo 13*, we got to watch the re-enactment of Mission Control in Houston struggle with fulfilling their unique purpose of not only getting people into outer space, but doing everything in their power to ensure their safe return back to earth.

There's a common debate about what to talk about first, mission or vision. Do whatever makes the most sense to your group. In general, focus on the vision first; look at the end result you're trying to achieve and then explore your mission or purpose in accomplishing that end result. However, there are times when the mission is really your group's immediate concern, and you may prefer to use it as a starting point for discussions.

Consider a community task force that is charged to hire a new recreation director. The group might want to start with clarifying their mission; what they were directed to do within certain parameters (such as the maximum salary that could be offered). Following this conversation, they could naturally proceed to discuss their vision: the kind of recreation program the community wishes to create or sustain and the characteristics and qualifications of a director who would satisfy that end result.

Clarifying a mission isn't complicated, but groups must make the time and effort to talk with one another and reach agreements. The *collective* agreement on a group's purpose is central to determining the framework for what people will actually do as part of their everyday work.

For example, let's say a school board's mission is to set policy and provide overall direction for the school district. That statement implies a great deal in terms of where the board will put their time and effort. At the group level, it really tells the individual members what they should/should not be doing. It says that they will set policy and determine overall district goals, but they will not tell the superintendent how to implement the policy and goals on a day-to day basis. Micro-management of the central office staff and teachers is not their purpose, collectively or individually. Simply put, every time the school board meets, their focus (and the outcomes and agenda for their meetings) should be toward fulfilling their mission.

Words can be subtle, yet powerful, in setting boundaries for the group. It is critical that the wording in mission statements is clear and can be understood by all who work within the group or groups affected by them. Consider a customer relations department within an organization. It could be that the department's mission is to provide leadership, overall direction, and support for improved customer service efforts. On the other hand, it could be that the mission is to coordinate and provide organizational accountability for improved customer service. One statement implies focus, guidance, and assistance while the other implies responsibility and accountability for results. Neither statement is good or bad. The important point is that each of these missions will result in very different actions in terms of where and how employees spend their time, energy, and financial resources.

It may be that the customer relations department never really engaged in a collective conversation about their mission, and therefore, there is no consistency among those employees as to their specific organizational purpose. And if there's no consistency among the customer relations department, imagine the confusion for others outside of the department. These outside folks don't know if the customer relations department is there to provide supervisory oversight or direction.

Another possibility is that someone in the customer relations department drafted a mission statement that is currently posted by the duplicating machine, but everyone knows "it's just a bunch of words that no one pays attention to." Once again, the power is in the group conversational process that includes discussions and collective agreements. Forget the fancy language—it's the *intent* behind the words that holds the power.

Although these conversations may sometimes prove difficult for those engaged in them (there are benefits and unique challenges to diverse opinions), in the long run they pay off. Within a group, a shared understanding of mission allows for clarity of purpose and actions. In addition, when people are able to maintain a focused approach toward the critical aspects of their work, there's less emotional energy spent being confused, angry, or frustrated.

● **CONVERSATION #3:**
VALUES

Trigger Questions:

- Why do I personally value being a member of this group/ organization?

- What are our collective core values?

- How do our core values relate to the way we treat each other and deliver services to our customers?

Values hold extraordinary power for both individuals and groups. A value can be defined as a principle, standard, or quality considered inherently worthwhile or desirable. In essence, our core values are the internal drivers of our external behaviors.

Workgroups who talk about and demonstrate their core values among themselves and those they serve experience a remarkable cohesiveness and shared dedication for their work. They are able to maintain their commitment and efforts for sometimes less financial compensation, because they place such a high value on what they do. Look at the number of people who devote endless hours of volunteer time, energy, and expertise to worthwhile endeavors. What draws these people together? Usually it's a shared value system.

Consider the man or woman who prepares and serves food for the homeless. There are many people who have done this with compassion and love week after week, year after year. They work with other volunteers who despite ethnic, income, and religious differences share the value of helping others who are less fortunate. The wonderful by-product is that when our behaviors are in line with our values we experience a deep sense of purpose and meaning in our actions. It makes us feel good about what we're doing!

The importance of shared values carries over into the traditional workplace as well. I once facilitated a meeting with a group of highly trained and experienced social workers. As they shared with each other why they personally valued their work, I was struck not only by the intensity of their words but the feelings behind them. They were individually and collectively *passionate* about meeting their clients' needs. Money (although everyone needed to earn a living) was not the main factor that drove them. It was the ability to serve their clients in an appropriate and compassionate manner that was most important. On the other hand, this same workgroup became frustrated (to the point where several people resigned) when they felt the overall organization they worked for did not hold similar values and was not supportive in supplying the resources necessary for the social workers to provide quality services.

It seems that more than any other fundamental conversation, it is critical that an *individual's* core (meaning most important and non-negotiable) values be compatible with the group's *collective* values. If an individual can't come to terms with the collective organizational mindset and behaviors regarding values, he or she will find it difficult to work in that environment.

For instance, I have spoken with numerous health care providers (physicians, nurses, technicians) who have shared their anguish and fear about providing less than quality health care because their bosses placed a higher value on cost savings. One woman described how she felt she was literally being torn apart because she was not providing the standard of care that was necessary for her patients. Her personal values kept colliding with the organizational values, causing a very real battle to rage within her.

There was a young man I sat next to on a plane who had worked as a sales representative for a prestigious consulting firm. The firm espoused honesty, but in fact, the man was expected to make promises to customers that he knew could not be delivered. He described how he would wake up at night with cold sweats because this behavior was so far removed from how he viewed himself and his values. He ended up changing jobs to another company for less money, but with his values intact.

Our words can become particularly cheap when it comes to values. Some organizations tend to trivialize such things as quality, community, respect, professionalism, teamwork, or integrity. To make our words count, we need to continually build a shared understanding with one another about what these words mean on a day-to-day basis as we interact with our customers, make decisions, and allocate resources. To uncover our differences and build a shared commitment to our values takes real work. When we actually are able to dig below the surface, the results can be astounding!

For example, there were two organizations in the same community that provided similar services to veterans. Between the two groups was a history of distrust, anger, and finger pointing. At one time they had worked as two completely separate organizations, but as resources diminished and political pressures increased, the leadership of both organizations realized that, if the two groups continued to butt heads, the available funding dollars might diminish and veterans were going to suffer. Leadership decided the two staffs should come together to discuss their shared interests and mutual concerns.

The first joint meeting started out with a lot of tension. The tables and chairs were arranged in a circular fashion and people had mostly seated themselves with their own kind—those they worked with on a regular basis. There was a lot of silence and little eye contact among the participants. People were civil but barely so.

After an initial overview of the meeting outcomes and procedures, each person shared with the group their own core values and why they, as individuals, valued their work. What followed was powerful. Words can't adequately describe the shift that occurred in the room as people shared their feelings. The ice had melted, and for the first time everyone was able to see the others as genuine, caring human beings, not merely as frozen, self-serving manipulators.

There were two major reasons for this melting. First, the conversation was obviously quite authentic. Because participants felt so strongly about their work, they were more open to sharing. Because it was personal, people were able to quickly get beyond meaningless platitudes. Second, it became apparent right away that the people in the room had more commonalities than differences. Through their discovery of shared values, the door was now opened for further conversations.

The groups did not instantly resolve all their differences. But they were able to discuss and work toward mutual agreements on some very difficult issues. Deciding who would do what to better serve the veterans was tough and painful but their shared values proved to be their stabilizing force. When things became especially challenging, they were able to bring themselves back to the shared values to give them the common ground, strength, and courage to continue with their conversations and agreements.

● CONVERSATION #4:
CUSTOMERS

Trigger Questions:

• Who are our most important internal and external customers?

• What are our customers' needs and/or expectations?

• How well are we currently serving our customers? What are the gaps between what the customers want versus what we provide?

Conversations about customers and their needs are incredibly basic, and yet they frequently aren't discussed among co-workers. During fundamental conversations, it's important to consider the needs of both internal customers (those you work with to provide the service or product to others) and external customers (those you provide the service or product for).

As we do our work, we often attend more to our own needs or what we perceive our customers' needs are, rather than using our customers' perspectives and opinions as the focal point. When I was a teenager and would make my mother's birthday cake, I would make a chocolate cake, not because it was my mother's favorite (she actually preferred lemon meringue pie) but because it was what I liked the best. The funny thing about it was that I don't remember deliberately refusing to give her what she wanted. I simply didn't consider that her preferences might be different from mine. I was unable to shift from my own way of thinking into hers.

As we perform our work, it's important to *collectively* shift from our own ways of thinking to our customers' ways of thinking. This requires an awareness that the people we work with and those external to the workgroup are, in fact, customers with specific needs and requirements. Our job includes trying to meet those needs and requirements.

Sometimes though, it's hard to recognize the customer relationships that exist, particularly when it's with those with whom we work on a regular basis. For example, if I'm an employee, my boss is really my customer. If I'm president of the local historical society, the members are my customers. If I'm part of a surgical team, both my patient and co-workers are my customers, and if I serve on a volunteer committee, the other members are my customers. Although it sounds a bit odd to consider my own mother a customer when I made her birthday cake, in the context of this discussion, that's what she was.

The idea of customer-focused thinking (or lack of it) is quite obvious in some situations. When you purchase something in a store, you expect to be treated in a certain manner. If, for example, you have to argue with a sales clerk in order to return a barbecue grill that you couldn't assemble because it was missing essential parts, you can quickly see that business's lack of customer focus.

When you view things through your customers' eyes, you can no longer assume that your customers want what you want to give them or that they're lacking the competence to make decisions about what they really do want. Without a customer-oriented mindset, you can't do business successfully. And if you can't anticipate and meet your customers' needs, someone else will.

When I worked as a program coordinator at a health care education center, the staff regularly surveyed our customers about their educational needs. These customers were hospital personnel such as physicians, nurses, technicians, management, etc., located at different hospitals within a geographic area. The concept sounded terrific. What could be better than asking those you serve what educational support they needed and wanted?

The only problem was, we didn't listen. Instead, we continued to provide what we thought they needed (which was some darn good stuff, but wasn't what they had asked for). As a result, we educators were perceived as having an "egghead" mentality, incapable of responding to our customers' requests for educational training and development programs.

Eventually, we restructured the process for gathering information and fulfilling requests to make it more customer-focused. Representatives from both the education center and the individual hospitals worked collaboratively to develop a more relevant way to both gather information and deliver educational services so that it was aligned with each hospital's overall mission and strategic goals. As a result, our customers became increasingly satisfied with our services.

In recent years, the entire health care community in this country has undergone a major transition regarding customer service. Frequently, medical staff presumed they knew and understood all the needs of patients better than the patients themselves. "How could the patient possibly know what he or she needed?" was, and sometimes still is, a commonly held belief.

Even though most patients do not possess the knowledge, experience, or skill base of the health care providers, they do have specific expectations of how they want to be treated. They want to be cared for in a humane, dignified, compassionate, and professional manner.

Patients also have expectations in terms of access to information. They want to be able to communicate with a designated physician or nurse. They want to understand what is being said to them in a way that the technical jargon makes sense. They also have opinions about their bodies, and the patients and their families frequently want to be partners in making the decisions that will greatly influence their future.

As the competition among health care providers escalated, and accrediting bodies pushed for hospitals to respond to patients' needs and expectations, dramatic changes began to occur. For example, when my husband had exploratory surgery, he went to an outpatient clinic of the community hospital, conveniently located by our home. The waiting room was bright and comfortable with couches, TVs, current magazines, and fresh flowers. Almost immediately, he was ushered into the surgical area by a nurse who introduced herself and then served as our health care liaison until we left the building. She addressed him as Mr. Williams and outlined how things would proceed for the remainder of his visit.

While seated in the waiting room, I was offered fresh coffee and a coupon for a free pastry from the cafeteria. Joe and I talked with the physician before and after the tests. All of the health care workers were professional and caring. Everything was performed in a timely manner. We left the clinic with a clear understanding of my husband's recovery and medication instructions, whom to call with questions, and when the follow-up appointment was scheduled.

What the patients and their families needed and wanted as soon as they entered this clinic was clearly well thought out. As a result of those first impressions, my husband and I automatically perceived that the *overall* quality of the clinic and competency of the health care workers were excellent, even though we didn't have precise data to support those perceptions.

Although many large companies use extensive survey techniques to identify their customers' expectations, it need not always be a complicated, expensive process. Consider the owner of a small graphic arts business. As the graphic artist works with her client to design a product, it's only natural for her to seek out the client's desires and expectations, not only for the product itself, but also for delivery deadlines, fees, and how things will be handled if rework is required.

Once again, any group or organization that is customer-oriented has an attitude (and takes actions to back it up) that their reason to be is to serve their customers. They value their customers' opinions and recognize that in order to serve their customers they must provide them what they want, need, or expect.

For example, let's say a school board is getting ready to advertise an opening for a new superintendent. If they wanted to be sensitive to their customers (parents, teachers, students, etc.), they would hold open discussion groups within the community to ask the question, "What kind of qualities and qualifications should we be looking for in a new superintendent?" The school board could then develop a set of hiring criteria that was based on their customers' requirements rather than just their opinions of what was important.

Most people recognize that valuing *external* customers is good business but understanding and honoring *internal* customer needs is equally important. People who work together on a regular basis often fail to treat one another as customers. Unless we take time to talk with each other, it's hard to appreciate just how interconnected most of our jobs are to one another and how much one person's behaviors and actions can influence the delivery or quality of another person's work. There are often a lot of sincere "I never realized that" comments when people who work together actually sit down and discuss what it takes to get their jobs done and what happens when they don't get what they need.

Consider the conversation of a workgroup discussing how to prevent a backlog from occurring in the duplication/shipping department of a training organization that reproduced various educational support materials, including instructional binders, pamphlets, videos, and CDs. The folks in duplicating/shipping were going crazy with what they viewed as too much work and not enough people to do the job. The rest of the team was unaware of the severity of the problem because the duplicating staff always managed to assemble and ship the materials on time, although they had to work overtime or pull in additional workers to meet the deadline.

The workgroup, having representation from key areas of the staff involved in this work process, met to discuss the challenges of the duplication staff. The desired outcome of the workgroup was to develop a process where the end products (completed binders, etc.) were error-free and shipped in a timely manner. Of equal importance was that the stress level of the duplicating staff be reduced. In other words, there was no need for chaos in the duplicating room to be the norm rather than a rarity.

The group kept the discussion simple. They started out asking each member involved in the process what they needed to do their job. They asked each other questions that broadened their understanding of one another's work. They also determined what data they needed in order to get a more accurate picture of the situation, like how many times during the last month the duplicating machine had broken down in the middle of a job. As the discussions progressed, it became evident that the duplicating staff could not do their jobs without certain requirements. What they asked for was not unreasonable by the group's standards: such things as (1) a heads-up regarding project scope and timelines early on in the work; (2) paper, binders, and copier supplies available when needed; (3) functional, high speed equipment; (4) training in basic copier repair to reduce equipment downtime; (4) established checkpoints in the duplicating process for necessary quality control; (5) ample work space to assemble and ship materials; (6) regular opportunities to provide suggestions to program coordinators for specific ways to increase efficiency; and (7) accurate addresses and site locations for shipping. Through a series of conversations about internal customer requirements, the workgroup was able to significantly increase their delivery speed and efficiency, while decreasing their error rate, overtime, and stress level.

Realistically, it's not always possible to meet your customer's expectations or requirements. Sometimes additional human, financial, or technological resources just aren't available at a particular time. But that's no excuse not to make an effort to understand the customer's perspective, meet whatever expectations are immediately possible, and continue to create ways to meet or exceed remaining expectations.

● **CONVERSATION #5:**

PLANNING

Trigger questions:

- Where are we now? (What's happening that we need to pay attention to?)

- Where are we headed? (As we work to fulfill our vision, mission, and values and meet our customer requirements, where should we focus our efforts? What are our priorities?)

- How will we get there? (What actions do we need to take to accomplish our priorities? What are our timelines and who is responsible? What resources do we need? How will we measure success? How will we communicate, coordinate, and monitor our efforts?)

With planning conversations, all three trigger questions should be dealt with on an ongoing and regular basis. In concert with the vision, mission, values, and customer expectations, the planning questions create a structure and a process for putting general ideas into concrete form.

Think of it as if you were building a house. You would start with the end result; an idea of what you want your house to look like. You hire an architect, whose mission is to take your requirements (aluminum siding exterior, open floor plan, fireplace, four bedrooms, etc.) and create a blueprint. Then you hire a general contractor, whose mission is to direct and coordinate the various subcontractors to build the house. In order to do that, the contractor must create a plan. He has to estimate the dollar cost and establish priorities. He has to figure out who needs to do what, how much it will cost, when it needs to occur, and in what order. The land has to be cleared and the foundation laid before the house can be framed and the roof put on. As the subcontractors do their individual work, they must continually talk with the general contractor and refer to the blueprints to make sure that what they do is in sync with everyone else. If you decide you want a three-car instead of a two-car garage, you need to communicate that to the general contractor, who needs to notify the subcontractors whose work will be impacted by the change.

Planning conversations among co-workers should follow a similar process. Just as in building a house, we need to get a clear blueprint of what we're trying to achieve. Conversations about vision, mission, values, and customer requirements actually serve as the groundwork for planning conversations. Planning then provides the structure and process for bringing it all together. Like the general contractor, we must incorporate the budget, priorities, actions, timelines, and assignment of tasks into a plan.

When a well-thought-out plan is shared and understood, there's a tremendous synergy that occurs among co-workers. Individuals are more able to focus their time, energy, and/or money toward the collective priorities.

In *Sacred Hoops, Spiritual Lessons of a Hardwood Warrior* by Phil Jackson and Hugh Delehanty, Jackson described his head coaching experiences with the Chicago Bulls and his philosophy and plan for developing a professional sports team. He believed that selflessness and compassion are just as important to the team's development as winning. In Chicago, those concepts became part of a carefully devised game plan that molded highly talented, individual players (including Michael Jordan, Scottie Pippen, Toni Kukoc, Dennis Rodman, and others) into a cohesive team. Jackson called this strategy "mindful basketball"—acting with a clear mind, aggressiveness without anger or violence, respecting the enemy, living in the moment, and staying calm in the midst of chaos.

There was power in Jackson's focus toward three major priorities—winning, teamwork, and mindful basketball. He didn't just say, "Okay guys, our goal is to win. Now let's do it." He outlined a plan of action in very concrete terms for how they would work together to achieve their priorities. Equally important, he shared that information with his players regularly so that they were able to continually focus their efforts in that direction as well. The real power came from not just one person (Phil Jackson) but everyone (the team) moving in the same direction toward common goals. The game plan only worked when everyone had the same information and shared the same plan for moving ahead.

However, not everyone is interested in putting together plans in their day-to-day lives in order to better accomplish tasks. For a couple I knew who went on a family vacation every year, the act of planning the vacation became an ongoing source of conflict. The wife loved planning. She spent hours pouring over brochures and promotional material. Once the family had agreed on a location, she would prepare a day-by-day schedule of activities. She could pinpoint, almost to the hour, where the family would be and what they would be doing. To her, planning made sense. With advance reservations, she could take advantage of better rates and availability for airlines, hotels, and special events. Planning provided a structure and direction that actually helped her enjoy the vacation more. She felt that once she left home to start the vacation she could totally relax because everything was in place for a good time.

On the other hand, her husband preferred spontaneity. His idea of a vacation was to figure out where the family was going, scan the brochures on the plane, arrive at their destination, and allow the vacation to "emerge." His philosophy was that advance planning and scheduling was too confining and limiting. How did he know what he wanted to be doing on Wednesday at 1:00 p.m. of his vacation week? From his perspective, too much planning meant closing out possibilities and on-the-spot opportunities.

After a few years of this planning versus spontaneity tension during vacation time, they figured out a workable solution. The wife would continue her planning frenzy, but she would also build do-nothing days into the schedule. That way she could still be comfortable that the family would have time to enjoy the major attractions they wanted to see and not miss out on something that required advance reservations. Just as important, the husband wouldn't feel that he always had to be somewhere. By scheduling the do-nothing days, they allowed for more open-ended time to relax or be spontaneous.

Workgroups face a similar dilemma when developing a plan to focus and prioritize their efforts. Some people find planning to be a useful structure; others find it too confining and rigid. People tend to think it's an either-or situation when in fact it requires a more holistic approach. A good plan needs to provide structure and direction, and the planning process itself needs to be dynamic enough to adjust to emerging situations. Given today's fast pace and our continual access to new information and technology, we should expect and actually build into the planning process opportunities to make adjustments.

Conversations about planning can also help mobilize and position a group or organization for the future. Consider a hospital whose customer service scores ranked among the lowest in the country. At a strategic planning session, leadership and staff representing various hospital departments determined that improving customer service, and thereby raising the customer service scores, should become a hospital-wide priority. That priority was shared with the entire staff. Everyone, at all levels of the organization, was expected to direct their efforts toward the accomplishment of this goal. Two years later, the hospital had significantly raised customer service scores. This would never have been possible without a collective focus and effort.

The planning process doesn't have to be all-consuming, particularly with smaller businesses or workgroups. Once again, the power is in the actual conversations and the mutual agreements reached among co-workers about where to collectively place their resources of time, energy, and money. The implementation of these ideas becomes part of everyone's ongoing work.

So for example, a team of sixth-grade teachers might determine that their three priorities for the upcoming school year are to further incorporate technology with student learning, develop students' conflict resolution skills, and raise student math scores. Part of their game plan should include ways to incorporate these priorities into the everyday curriculum. All sixth-grade teachers would continue their separate teaching responsibilities (and their own individual priorities), but always looking and acting toward the collective priorities.

Another planning group might involve a small, local police department. They would discuss, "Where are we now?"—meaning, how well are we doing in terms of meeting our vision, mission, values, and customer requirements? They might discuss the increase in juvenile arrests, or huge technological advances that could help them become more effective and efficient in their work, or the lack of cooperation and interface between them and schools, social service agencies, and the health care community in dealing with children's issues.

Let's assume that as a result of this planning conversation, the officers determine that their collective priorities for the next year are to (1) purchase state-of-the-art computer equipment; (2) increase the staff's computer technology skills; and (3) enhance relationships within the community. By setting these priorities, they are saying they will continue to conduct their daily duties as police officers while at the same time placing a special emphasis on the agreed-upon collective priority areas. In the end, everyone should have a clear understanding of the game plan in terms of what they are doing, how and when they are doing it, who is doing what, and what they will view as measures of success.

● CONVERSATION #6:
ROLES/RESPONSIBILITIES

Trigger Questions:

• Who is responsible for what and when?

• What are our processes for doing our work? At what points do we interface with one another, and how can we do that in an efficient and cooperative manner?

• What skills and expertise does each of us bring to the table? In what ways can we best take advantage of these skills and expertise?

Conversations among co-workers about roles and responsibilities are challenging. "It's where the rubber meets the road," in that we're no longer talking at a big picture level. When we talk about people's roles and responsibilities, we're looking at what each individual does or will do in relation to the whole. Even though the conversation focuses on the roles and responsibilities within a particular *position*, it's still a *person* who is doing the work. Any changes or adjustments must be made not only at the group level but at a personal one as well. That's where the real challenge lies.

Most people who work together have a general sense of who's supposed to do what. It's either in writing (job description or diagram of work flow) or has been communicated verbally at some time. But until these descriptions are discussed and agreed upon *collectively* by the folks who work together, they really are the *individuals'* perceptions and assumptions. One person's idea of her roles and responsibilities may be very different from how others view her roles and responsibilities.

Co-workers are particularly susceptible to confusion about roles and responsibilities during times of corporate mergers, re-engineering, and reorganization. These changes are happening more frequently. A man sitting next to me on an airplane described how he was just returning from a meeting where his colleagues were trying to clarify and reduce hostility and frustration about their roles and responsibilities. There had been a recent corporate merger, but "Jim" had been told business would proceed as usual, at least at his end. Then he started getting e-mails from someone he'd never talked to, or even heard of, telling him what he was supposed to do. He called his boss (already at another location) to ask what was going on and to request a meeting of the key players. Jim discovered that as a result of the merger, several positions had been redefined and consolidated. Amazingly, management had failed to notify the individuals involved about the changes and how these changes would impact their work. The man sending Jim the e-mails was actually part of the new management team now directing one aspect of Jim's job.

According to Jim, the meeting had been valuable. He was surprised at how just getting together and discussing the issues made such a difference in people's perceptions and understanding. Although he knew that discussions would need to continue, he felt satisfied that they had been able to delineate their roles and responsibilities with one another. Jim wasn't particularly opposed to the new way of organizing the business (he still had a similar job and responsibilities), but he was disappointed by the fact that this meeting hadn't occurred earlier. A great deal of confusion, anxiety, and inefficiency could have been avoided.

The goal of role and responsibility conversations is to walk away with a precise understanding of, and agreement about, who does what and when in order to accomplish the vision, mission, values, and priorities of the organization or workgroup. As is often stated, "the devil's in the details," and this fundamental conversation is designed to work out those details through skillful discussion and negotiation among co-workers. The larger and more spread out the organization, the more complex the conversations become. And the more entrenched the individuals are in particular ways of thinking and doing business, the more difficult it is to problem-solve collaboratively.

Consider the health care organization that experienced a major restructuring. The program staff at corporate headquarters had a history of having a great deal of responsibility, authority, and resources. They had set policy and directed, implemented, and monitored various programs for their branch organizations throughout the United States. Following the restructuring, these programs were decentralized from headquarters with the funding dollars and the authority to direct those dollars to be handled at a regional level.

So now, on the one hand, there were these highly competent, knowledgeable people at the headquarters level whose role had changed from that of directors (with responsibility, authority, and funding power) to consultants (providing expertise, setting overall policy, and offering recommendations to the regions and branch facilities). On the other hand, the people at the regional level were now given the decision-making, implementation, and funding authority to better meet their regional and local needs.

As a result of these changes in roles and responsibilities, there was a great deal of confusion about who was doing what, how, and when. Recognizing that this confusion was causing duplication of efforts, mismanagement of resources, and a lack of quality service to their customers, representatives from the groups set up a series of meetings to clarify and discuss their new roles and responsibilities and how they could work better together for the good of the organization. In planning for the meetings, they recognized problem-solving would be difficult while people were still jockeying for positions of power and imbedded in their own ways of thinking. Therefore, during the initial meeting, the bulk of time was spent focusing on current realities and mutual interests, rather than on any specific problem-solving.

This wasn't intended to be a single "feel good" interaction. To succeed, this collaborative effort required conversations and agreements among the key players for many months and years to come. Unfortunately, the conversations and relationship building did not continue and any strides toward collaboration were made only at an individual level—one-on-one. Therefore, the full potential and power of the two groups to work together did not occur.

Formal conversations about roles and responsibilities can be challenging. There are often a number of legitimate concerns like, "We don't have the time, it may not be worth the effort, or all hell will break loose if we confront our areas of disagreement." However, experience tells us that until co-workers are able to have these conversations they will endure a workplace with undercurrents of inefficiency, confusion, anxiety, and frustration. The ability of groups to discuss and resolve role and responsibility issues in a way that maintains individuals' dignity are skills worth developing and practicing. A group can achieve amazing things when they are focused and committed toward this effort.

As an illustration, there was a federal organization that provided

training, consultation, and support materials for hospital personnel as it related to clinical information management. This
eight-year-old office started out with only three employees and
jumped to forty (about a third of them off site) within five years.
It was a fast-paced organization with lots of priorities of equal
importance and little lead-time to accomplish them. Trying to
satisfy their customers (located at over 170 hospitals across the
country) while staying ahead of the technological learning curve
was a daily challenge for this training center. When new people
were hired, they were expected to hit the ground running.

The individuals who worked at this office did outstanding work.
There were educational program coordinators and assistants,
media/technology specialists, office automation clerks, and
administrative support staff working toward similar goals. They
were known as doers, able to respond rapidly to external customer demands. Yet internally, the cost of doing business at this
pace was taking its toll. It seemed that everyone was in crisis
management mode most of the time and frequently at each
other's throats in the process. As a group, they felt they could be
even more efficient and productive, with less stress and frustration, if people had a shared understanding of who was supposed
to do what and when. They already had written job descriptions
and a general sense, by way of observation and experience, of
how the work should flow through the organization. However,

there were a lot of gray areas where it was unclear who had what responsibilities.

When the staff had consisted of three, loosely defined roles and responsibilities worked well. They could self-correct as the work was in progress and quickly make adjustments on an as-needed basis. Now, the staff was larger, and the products and services they provided required more complex systems of people and technology working together. The staff needed structure but only enough to provide guidance and clarity. They also needed flexibility—they knew full well that, because of their custom-ers' unique needs, their work rarely followed a precise pattern. I was hired to help the staff develop internal guidelines, including work processes describing recommended scenarios for how the work should move through the organization. The effort was also to include the clarification of roles and responsibilities of staff for each phase of the work.

Every person participated in a cross-sectional workgroup over a one-year period. Workgroups were formed on the basis of five core products and services the organization provided their customers. Both internal and external customer requirements were identified. The groups reviewed the way their work was currently conducted and examined potential breakdown and bottleneck areas. From this data, each group created an optimal way of doing business, and guidelines were created with rec-ommended workflow processes. Staff had the opportunity to collectively review, discuss, and make necessary adjustments to the guidelines before implementation. During the pilot phase of implementation, the workgroups monitored the effectiveness of the interim guidelines and suggested refinements to their work processes.

What were the results of this effort? For one thing, the organization now had baseline information and expectations for current and new staff about their internal work processes. Staff members had a shared understanding of their roles and responsibilities. They also had agreements among one another that when a work process had to be altered (and it frequently did), they would communicate and negotiate timelines with everyone whose work was impacted by the changes. Workgroups were expected to share their progress and improvement efforts with the entire organization, thus clarifying for external customers who they could go to for information and services. These were new expectations for staff behavior, and the reward and recognition system was redesigned to encourage these behaviors.

As this example demonstrates, in order for fundamental conversations to be of benefit, they must be ongoing. Because of the ever-changing realities of our work, these agreements are rarely set in stone. But once baseline understanding and agreements have been reached, they become a reference point for future discussions.

This group's goal was to eventually reach a point where these conversations wouldn't be considered as special or unusual, they would just be a part of what you did in order to get the work accomplished effectively and efficiently. The staff was striving to accomplish something far greater then just the establishment of clearly defined roles and responsibilities. They were in the process of evolving their group into one with the capacity and skill to engage in all kinds of relevant conversations.

● CONVERSATION #7:
DEAL BUSTERS

Trigger Questions:

- How will we communicate with one another?

- How will we resolve conflict?

- How will we make decisions?

- How can we best provide support and demonstrate appreciation for one another?

As group members discuss and agree upon deal busters, they are really looking one another in the eye and saying, "Okay, here's the deal. If we're going to work together, there are some things we need to get straight with one another or our relationship won't fly."

When co-workers engage in deal buster conversations, they're establishing acceptable behaviors for working together. How well co-workers communicate, resolve conflict, make decisions, and provide support and appreciation can significantly affect the outcome of their collective work.

Deal buster issues are like icebergs; their potential to do damage lies beneath the surface. Ignore them at your peril. By putting deal buster issues on the table for group discussions, we elevate them to a place of visibility and importance, where they can be dealt with *before* major damage occurs.

Deal buster agreements are absolutely critical. Workgroups tend to become dysfunctional if they don't have them. Without such agreements, the best-case scenario is confusion and chaos among co-workers about who is doing what and when. The worst-case scenario is when the whole system breaks down and it becomes impossible to provide a quality service or product.

Realistically, how can people work effectively with one another if they don't have agreed-upon methods for communicating important issues and information? How can they make unified decisions unless they have agreed-upon ways of reaching them? How will they be able to confront areas of disagreement directly and follow expected protocols for resolving differences if they haven't mutually set these expectations in advance? And finally, how can they appreciate and support one another in their work if they've never talked about what support and appreciation look like in real terms?

Deal buster agreements hold so much power and have such far-reaching effects because they are grounded in trust. When co-workers see each other making an effort to honor these agreements, it goes a long way toward building tolerance and respect. They are motivated to support and appreciate one another. When mistakes are made, they're more likely to forgive and are able to move into a problem-solving mode with greater speed.

Conversely, when deal buster agreements are broken, people feel violated; they feel as if they've been back-stabbed. When this occurs, co-workers are less likely to have faith and trust in one another. They will be less motivated to speak kindly of certain individuals in the presence of others. They will be less likely to share information. They will be unwilling to go the extra mile when called upon. And most of all, they will do whatever they can to build a wall of protection so that they are not violated again. Surviving, rather than thriving, becomes the mental model that drives their work. A broken trust can take years to heal.

In most instances, there's no sordid conspiracy occurring in the workplace that prevents co-workers from discussing and reaching these deal buster agreements. More likely, people are so busy doing their work, they just don't think about the ramifications of not having them. Often co-workers assume that everyone shares the same understanding about "acceptable" behaviors and practices.

Unfortunately, deal buster conversations usually don't take place unless there's a crisis of some sort, and by that time, there are a lot of emotions attached to an issue. Better to discuss and reach agreements when a working relationship is first formed and then periodically monitor how well these agreements are working.

Deal buster agreements should be simple and concrete. For example, my friend Mary Ann and I were considering buying a horse trailer together. We realized that by purchasing the trailer jointly, we could get a newer model and save quite a bit of money. Before we entered into this mutual purchase, we felt it was important to set parameters for maintaining and using the trailer.

We did some "How should we handle this?" planning with one another and came up with the following: We will evenly split the financial costs for the trailer purchase, yearly insurance, and maintenance. The trailer will be kept at my house. I'll pay to have the driveway enlarged to accommodate the trailer. Mary Ann will coordinate the insurance purchase and trailer maintenance. She'll drive when we trailer our horses long distances because her vehicle has stronger towing power; otherwise we'll take turns driving. If one of us no longer wants the trailer, she will allow the other person the opportunity and time to buy her out at market price. Otherwise, the trailer will be sold and the money equally divided. No one else has permission to use the trailer, other than the two husbands, without each other's approval. If either of us has a problem with how we're handling the agreements or have other issues that need to be discussed, we'll talk directly with one another about it. We will provide support to each other by working together to hook up, load horses, and clean and maintain the trailer. If one person has less time available, the other person will take up the slack. At some other time, the favor will be returned.

To think or expect that every potential contingency can be identified and outlined is unreasonable. The intent is to explore individual parameters and reach mutual agreements. As these agreements are followed, trust builds, along with the capacity to problem-solve jointly when difficult issues arise that had not been previously anticipated.

In the workplace, the most powerful deal buster agreements tend to be equally concrete and simplistic. Although deal buster conversations are unique to each workgroup, the most frequent ones relate to communication, decision-making, conflict resolution, and support/appreciation issues.

● COMMUNICATION

In relation to communication agreements, there are three guidelines. People who work together should:

1. Develop a manageable communication system to share information and discuss important issues.

Without a manageable communication system, a group cannot expect to work cohesively as a team; it simply won't happen. Effective communication is more difficult than it seems, because for many co-workers, the opportunity to actually be in the same location at the same time is rare indeed. And for those who are together, most likely they're fully engaged in providing the actual service or product. Therefore, it's up to those who work together to come up with ways they can regularly touch base with one another.

To make this happen, we need structures and processes in place that make sense to individual workgroups. When we establish these systems, it's important to make distinctions about which system is appropriate under what circumstances. Routine information can easily be shared electronically. If there's a need for a problem-solving discussion, or if the information is more personal in nature, then a person-to-person interaction is more appropriate and effective.

In the workplace, information is power; without access to information, co-workers are unable to make data-driven decisions. As a result, it's sometimes difficult to know what and how much information to share with co-workers. People want to be kept informed, but too much information can be overwhelming. In general, people want to be kept in the know about information or issues that interface or impact their work. They hate being caught off guard or put in an embarrassing position because they weren't given the right information at the right time. Therefore, co-workers need to establish communication agreements.

Each individual should be responsible for considering who needs what information at what point in time, and then to make sure the right person gets it. You should also make sure that when problem-solving discussions occur, the right people have the opportunity to provide input. This common courtesy is a workplace necessity, and it deserves the individual and organizational commitment and discipline required to ensure that it happens.

2. **Take time to communicate with one another about important information and issues on a regularly scheduled and timely basis.**

Simply stated, co-workers must take the time to communicate with one another. In many cases, the problem isn't that communication systems aren't in place; people often just don't take the time or make the effort to use them. For some communications, sending an e-mail is sufficient, particularly when it is for information sharing. But in other cases, particularly when you have to make sure that all parties are on the same page, you have to talk with one another, even if it means having to shut down regular work operations, meet during lunch hour, or have evening meetings or phone conversations.

It's also a matter of shifting perspective. We've got to stop thinking of these interactions as being separate from our work because, in actuality, they're an integral part of our work. We must also get out of our individual work boxes and view our work from a larger, organizational perspective.

3. Make wise use of the group's time together.

Even though groups may have systems in place and take time to communicate with each other, communication will prove ineffective if the group is unable to make wise use of their time together. There's a reason most people will tell you that workplace meetings are often a waste of time. Frequently, when groups get together to share information and discuss issues there's a lack of clarity and conciseness to the conversations. Time limits aren't honored, and at the end of the meeting, people aren't clear about what, if anything, was decided.

If the only outcome is to share information, is the meeting even necessary? It's far more effective for group members to use meetings as a time for group discussion and problem-solving.

Outcome-based agendas, with a clear idea of what you want to see happen as a result of this meeting, should be developed and distributed in advance of the meeting. Where appropriate, written materials that help members become more knowledgeable about a particular issue should also be provided in advance. Everyone should be expected to read the materials before, rather than during, the meeting. Anyone presenting or sharing information during the meeting should clearly and concisely articulate the issue during a time-limited discussion. Following the discussion, a group member should summarize the conclusions, next steps, assignments, and feedback mechanisms to track or bring closure to the issue.

● CONFLICT RESOLUTION

The ability to constructively resolve conflict is critical for any workgroup. The benefits are great: greater understanding, trust, strengthening of the relationships, capacity to problem-solve, and energy to expend toward positive emotions and actions.

One problem is that people handle conflict differently. Some of us thrive on direct confrontation, but most of us go out of our way to avoid it. Many people don't want the hassles, particularly in the workplace, of dealing with others to resolve difficult issues, even though when conflict is handled appropriately it can be a positive problem-solving mechanism.

But resolving conflict can take time, effort, flexibility in thinking, and personal soul searching that are, for whatever reason, often in short supply. As a result, if someone is not interested in expending these required resources, they may resort to behaviors that come across as manipulative, self-serving, or downright deceitful.

In the context of deal buster agreements, most co-workers don't ask for much. What they don't want is to be side-stepped by others when an issue or difficulty emerges. If it directly relates to them, they want to be a part of the problem-solving process. A classic example involves manager #1 who doesn't like what manager #2 is doing. Rather than confront the issue directly with that person, he goes further up the supervisory chain to get the issue resolved. Possibly, if manager #1 had talked with manager #2 first, they might have been able to resolve their differences. Even if they had not, at least the effort was made by manager #1 to communicate. And that's where the trust builds. Initial contact opens the door for managers to make a joint appeal to a higher authority to reach resolution. The average person recognizes she isn't always going to get her way. What builds animosity in the workplace is when others aren't straight shooters in their approach.

● DECISION-MAKING

People want to know the rules of the game for decision-making. They want to know who has the power and authority to make what decisions, under what circumstances, and at what point in time. Most can abide by the outcome of a decision, even if they don't agree with it, but they want clarity about the process. Look at the election process in this country. We cast votes for our candidates; sometimes they win and sometimes they lose. As long as we view the process as fair and people play by the established rules, we accept the outcome and move on with our lives. However, if people perceive they've been misguided and fraud has occurred, then anger and a need for justice sets in.

Decision-making occurs at different levels, from having only input into a decision to being fully engaged in the decision-making process. People who work together need to be clear about if they have decision-making authority and, if so, determine what level of decision-making they will use and under what circumstances.

For example, a manager may need to make a decision on a particular issue. The manager may seek input from others before making the decision. Co-workers typically don't have a problem with that if, in fact, the manager is clear that it is only input she's seeking. If however, she implies to her subordinates that "we" need to make a decision and then proceeds to go against group recommendations, the group will respond with, "What the heck did you ask us for if you already had your mind made up?" They view the experience as a complete waste of time.

Besides clarity about levels of decision-making, every group of people who work together should talk about the way they will make their decisions—the process for how they will reach final agreements. These agreements will vary from group to group, depending on the nature of the work and the type of organization. Does a group require that they reach consensus (group members must at a minimum be able to support the final decision even if they don't personally agree with it) or is a majority vote acceptable? Are there circumstances when one method of reaching agreement is better than another? If so, what are they?

If a group fails to determine their method and time frame for reaching agreements, they will find themselves in decision limbo, unable to reach closure on decisions. They will leave meetings with a sense of confusion and frustration, thinking, "All we do is talk. How come we aren't able to bring closure to our discussions? This thing seems to drag on forever."

For a group to not make a decision about a particular issue is perfectly acceptable, as long as it's a conscious choice and there's a communication feedback loop in place to review the issue at some designated point. As with the other fundamental conversations, the benefit comes from the common *group* understanding and agreements, rather than *individual* preferences and actions. This is what keeps everyone moving in the same direction.

● SUPPORT AND APPRECIATION

When co-workers have support and appreciation conversations, they are raising their group awareness to a higher level. First, there's an acknowledgement that as humans we like to be supported and appreciated for our efforts. Second, we recognize that people tend to do more of the things they receive support and appreciation for. And finally, we gain an understanding that people have different preferences for giving and receiving support and appreciation.

Support and appreciation are different from rewards and recognition in that they tend to be less formalized and subtler. People don't expect to be rewarded or recognized for everything they do, especially if it's part of their everyday work. For example, a receptionist at a doctor's office is *expected* to be kind and courteous to patients. A high school principal is *expected* to attend evening school functions. A voluntary Cub Scout leader is *expected* to organize meetings and activities. These behaviors are simply part of the job requirements.

However, people do want (and we tend to forget this) to be supported and appreciated in their work. That support and appreciation can come in many forms, depending on individual preferences. An extraordinary example of this was the superintendent of schools from my hometown. In an effort to demonstrate her support for funding an elementary school expansion, she retired but then continued to serve as superintendent on a voluntary basis for a designated period of time, thus saving the district valuable dollars.

For most of us, demonstration of support and appreciation is far less dramatic but still very critical. For the receptionist, principal, and Cub Scout leader, a sincere and personal thank you by superiors and/or customers (be it patients, parents, or kids) for their efforts might be viewed as an act of appreciation. In terms of support, the receptionist might request that patient education materials be provided at the front desk to help her provide accurate information to patients. A principal might request additional community involvement in evening activities as a way of demonstrating support. The Cub Scout leader might request help from parents to chaperone a camping trip as a demonstration of support.

The important thing is to put support and appreciation "out there" as an ongoing conversation among those who work together. The only way we can know (not merely assume) how to support and appreciate each other is to ask. The very act of considering it important enough to talk about builds trust and cooperation.

Part Three

How Do We Go About Having These Conversations?

Thus far, this book has described the *why* (*Why* do we need to talk with one another?) and the *what* (*What* do we need to talk about?) as they relate to fundamental conversations in the workplace. This section talks about the *how;* how we actually go about having these conversations, keeping them focused, making them more than one-shot deals, and honoring the agreements as part of our day-to-day work.

To help gain an overall picture of how to use fundamental conversations in our working lives, consider the "conversation cycle." The conversation cycle is an overall framework for the fundamental conversations and a context for using the trigger questions.

If you think of fundamental conversations as part of an ongoing cycle, rather than as a singular event, it suggests that the work done prior to, during, and following the conversations are of equal importance. People are probably familiar with, and have used, many pieces and parts of the cycle; however, it's only when you see conversations as part of a whole cycle that there is genuine value and relevancy for its use in the workplace.

● THE CONVERSATION CYCLE

When co-workers start consciously using the conversation cycle, it may seem a bit awkward. That's why a step-by-step process can be helpful in serving as a reference for individuals and groups as they learn to think and behave in ways that encourage and support fundamental conversations.

The conversation cycle incorporates three phases. Whether the conversation is between two people or two hundred, it generally follows a similar process, although the level of formality, complexity, and amount of time involved are definitely influenced by the size of the group.

● PHASE #1:
Before the Conversation

1. A *thought* by one or more individuals that a fundamental conversation among co-workers would be beneficial

2. A *recommendation* by an individual(s) to initiate a fundamental conversation among co-workers

3. *Advance notice and/or buy-in* among co-workers for the conversation

● **PHASE #2:**
During the Conversation: the Trigger Questions

1. *Setting the framework* by introducing conversation purpose, outcomes, and trigger question(s)

2. Group members' *individual* responses to the trigger questions

3. *Group reflection, discussion,* and *understanding* of common themes and areas of agreement/disagreement

4. Further *group exploration* of similarities/differences and areas of mutual benefit

5. Initial *group agreements*

● **PHASE #3:**
Following the Conversation

1. *Honoring* of agreements with follow-through behaviors/ actions/redistribution of resources

2. Ongoing *feedback* (How are we doing and what have we learned?) and improvements (How do we make this better?)

Feedback from managers and co-workers who have used this conversation cycle claims it helps them be more thoughtful about when and how to approach and engage others. By thinking in advance about the conversation, they are better able to get colleagues' input and to facilitate constructive discussions that lead to working agreements. In addition, they are more likely to recognize that agreements and actions go hand-in-hand. It builds confidence and credibility among managers and co-workers to know they have the ability to talk with one another, reach agreements, and make things happen.

As we follow this cycle, it's important to keep in mind how much our own personal ways of thinking and behaving influence the process. Looking at how our thoughts and actions can affect the way the group conversations are conducted and the results that are achieved is much more difficult than following a step-by-step cookbook approach to the cycle. How we treat others and the environment we create during conversations are far more likely to make or break a group's ability to articulate and sustain their conversation efforts and agreements. At the core is trust.

When a person occasionally interrupts another person during a fundamental conversation, it certainly doesn't promote a healthy discussion. But in most cases, co-workers will give each other some leeway. We don't expect people to be perfect communicators all the time. But when there are misunderstandings among co-workers that relate to trust, it's as if a door slams shut. Trust goes into hiding and under cover. Along with trust goes creative thinking, fun, cooperation, and an interest in making things better. For people to keep that door shut and protected requires enormous energy that could be better spent working positively and productively.

Some of us have witnessed cases where, during a simulated training exercise, a person was able to follow a prescribed number of steps to communicate effectively. Back at the office, that same person used those steps with his workgroup during meetings, only to then violate the workgroup trust by misrepresenting their perspectives or confidences when he walked out the door. He followed the recipe for effective communication but failed because of his inability to inspire trust.

If we rely strictly on a cookbook approach to fundamental conversations, we're missing the point. In the cookbook approach, if the result turns out terrible, we're likely to blame the recipe, rather than the cook. That way the cook doesn't have to assume any personal responsibility for the results. Having a recipe is great as long as we remember that recipes aren't foolproof. The human element is critical in the equation of success.

● THE FOUR GUIDELINES

Having stressed how important it is to think beyond the cookbook approach, there are four guidelines that can help co-workers during their fundamental conversations:

(1) start with your own area of influence; (2) be aware of your intentions and their effect on conversations; (3) move to a state of attention; and (4) keep at it to keep it going. The guidelines are intended to encourage and enrich co-workers' use of the conversation cycle by offering suggestions that incorporate new ways of thinking, as well as techniques that support constructive behaviors.

First and foremost, we must look within—to examine our thoughts and actions and their impact on our co-workers and ourselves. Only then should we work to improve our various skill-building tools and techniques to enhance our conversation and follow-through efforts. With this inside-out approach, we create a foundation that is authentic and genuine on which to use our tools and techniques.

● **GUIDELINE #1:**

START WITH YOUR OWN AREA OF INFLUENCE

When I talk with colleagues or friends about the seven funda-mental conversations I often hear *but they . . .* excuses. Included are such things as, "I wish we could get together and talk about those things where I work or volunteer, but THEY will never go for it. I like the idea, but what can one person do when THEY don't care? We sure could use those conversations, but even if we do talk about this stuff, THEY will never change, so what's the use?"

My response to that is, "Forget about THEY, what about YOU?" What fundamental conversations do *you* need to initiate with co-workers to improve how you cooperatively conduct your work or support others in their work? One person won't be able to single-handedly change an entire volunteer organization or workplace. But one person *can* go a long way in influencing their immediate work surroundings.

When you explore your own areas of influence you raise aware-ness of and accept personal responsibility for your thoughts and actions and their impact on others; you recognize and honor your personal choices and power; and you use that power to influence (but not control) circumstances and people.

Looking within is tough work, particularly since most of us have been trained to problem-solve by finding logical answers and approaches outside ourselves. But when we really do "get it," when we really comprehend the personal responsibility we have and the power our influence holds, the results can be profound in terms of where we place our emotional and physical energy, how we relate to other people, and what we (individually and collectively) are able to accomplish.

A personal experience helped me come to terms with this guideline. Years ago, I was working as an educator in the area of leadership training and development. Our local office was filled with dissention and mistrust between the management and staff. Stephen Covey's book *The 7 Habits of Highly Effective People* had recently been published, and I attended a conference where Dr. Covey was one of the featured speakers. Because his words had such relevancy for me, as well as those I provided educational services for, I asked Dr. Covey for an interview for our organization's newsletter. He graciously accepted.

As we started the telephone interview, I was very much in an intellectual mindset. I was caught up in Dr. Covey's concepts and words. I loved the practical framework of the book. After all, what could be a clearer pathway to success than the description of seven habits of highly successful people? But then I asked a question related to a common theme I had heard for years, and his response quickly moved me from a level of detached observer to one of personal awareness. I asked him what you did if you worked with or for people who weren't competent, ethical, or considerate. His seven habits were impressive, but if you in fact worked with or for jerks, as many people claim they do, then were you off the hook? You'd have no choice but to either act like everyone else or give up and do everything possible to keep the trust door bolted.

Dr. Covey's response was straightforward. He described how the right approach is to focus on one's own circle of influence, which starts with raising awareness of our own thoughts and actions. When you assume responsibility for yourself, you in fact increase your own personal power. You spend your time and energy focusing on things you can do something about. When you focus on others' inadequacies or negative situations, you decrease your personal power, sinking into a blaming, victim mentality.

Suddenly this wasn't just intellectual bantering with a well-known and respected author. It was now personal. I saw myself in his words. True, he had given his readers a recipe of sorts by way of the seven habits: (1) be proactive; (2) begin with the end in mind; (3) put first things first; (4) think win/win; (5) seek first to understand, then to be understood; (6) synergize; and (7) sharpen the saw. But Dr. Covey was also saying that the seven habits only held their value if we were willing and able to assume personal responsibility. Using others as an excuse for our own thinking and behavior simply wasn't acceptable. We needed to put our thoughts and actions toward things we could do something about.

At that moment, it struck me how much of my workplace energy was spent focused on people and situations I could not change. I had become so accustomed to believing that I was powerless in the midst of the "madness" at my workplace that I had lost sight of the multitude of areas in which I had enormous influence and power. I was so into the mentality of, "nothing will ever change unless *they* get their act together" that I forgot about *my* role in creating this workplace drama. I forgot about the power of choice. I was choosing to use my energy in ways that were destructive rather than constructive, especially to me and those I worked with and for whom I truly cared.

Simply by consciously choosing to focus on things within my own area of influence, I felt my world change. By taking the inward approach of assuming personal responsibility for my thoughts and actions, I saw how I had contributed to the negativity of my workplace. Working on myself first, I built a foundation of personal integrity. I was then more able to effectively incorporate a variety of tools and techniques to help me work productively and collaboratively with others.

On a concrete level, that meant that when I was in a meeting with my bosses, I tried not to spend an ounce of energy judging or trying to change them. I de-personalized their behaviors, acknowledging that they had their own issues to deal with that had nothing to do with me. I allowed them to be whom they chose to be. I also determined they would not influence who I chose to be.

I worked hard to behave in ways that were consistent with my espoused core values, choosing to downplay the negative and accentuate the positive. I looked for ways to support the organization and those I worked with, including my bosses. That meant spending less time bad-mouthing and gossiping and more time with those interested in pursuing constructive discussions and agreements related to the fundamental conversations. Somewhere in this process, I became emotionally free to positively influence and impact those people and circumstances where I could really make a difference. The results were dramatic, both personally and professionally.

Fundamental conversations require us to focus our individual and collective energies in specific areas. There is absolutely no room for the victim mentality.

Practically speaking, as you rid yourself of the victim mentality, you also rid yourself of victim language. When you speak now, it is from a position of personal awareness, responsibility, power, and integrity. From this vantage point, your words are far more likely to be heard and valued by your co-workers. More importantly, you increase your own self-respect and confidence. This is what happens when you focus on your own areas of influence.

● **GUIDELINE #2:**

BE AWARE OF YOUR INTENTIONS AND THEIR EFFECT ON CONVERSATIONS

This guideline is also part of the solid foundation you need to create and sustain during any fundamental conversation effort. Similar to the previous guideline, becoming aware of your intentions and their effect on both the quality and outcome of conversations requires you to look within *before* you actively participate in conversations with co-workers.

An intention is a state of heart and mind about one's motivation, purpose, or reason for doing something. In making an intention, a specific direction for the behaviors and results that follow is set in motion. Similar to planting a seed in a garden, each seed establishes a particular pattern of growth. A corn seed is going to grow into a corn stalk and produce an ear of corn, not a tomato.

During fundamental conversations, we need to be aware that our intentions are like the kernel of corn. What we plant is what we get as the seed matures to its ripened state. Of course, a whole lot of other factors affect the results. In the case of both the corn and fundamental conversations, we must provide nourishment and a healthy environment to allow the seed to mature. Nevertheless, the intentions we plant as a predecessor to our conversations will have a direct relationship to the results we achieve with others.

As you participate in fundamental conversations, group members will be searching for your intentions. They're going to listen to your words and watch your actions. It's like those old western movies where the farmer catches a cowboy kissing his single daughter. As the farmer holds a gun to the cowboy, he growls something like, "What are your intentions with my daughter?" He's clearly implying that those intentions better be honorable (like marrying the young woman). He's going to listen to what the cowboy says and compare it with the cowboy's actions. They better jive or the cowboy is in *big* trouble.

That's what it's like in the workplace. When you suggest to co-workers that you want to initiate certain fundamental conversations, they're likely to look at you in a way that is very similar to how the farmer looked at the cowboy, only this time you're the cowboy! They're going to listen to what you say and then watch your behaviors. Your intentions better be honorable and they better be consistent with your current and future behaviors. Co-workers will know the difference, even if you fail to see these things yourself.

So what are honorable intentions as they relate to fundamental conversations? Perhaps it's more easily explained by looking at what *isn't* honorable: when you want to gain the cooperation of others for strictly self-serving purposes; when you want to use the conversations as a forum to manipulate, dominate, or control people and situations; when you start from a vantage point that it's the other guys who better get their act together; and this conversation is an opportunity to revise their way of thinking. None of these are honorable intentions, and they don't particularly inspire anyone to want to engage in fundamental conversations with us.

An honorable intention is to want to make something better for the good of all. What's in it for me may be involved, but there's also the aspect of what's in it for us and those we serve. There's openness and interest in other possibilities and perspectives that may be different from our current views.

A friend who's a medical technician shared a conversation she had with her boss. She had received her performance evaluation three weeks prior and was very unhappy with it. She felt it was unfair, unsubstantiated, and didn't represent her true work efforts. Even though she was angry about the whole thing, she decided (here's the intent) she was going to meet with her boss in an effort for each of them to better understand their perspectives and possibly reach some common understanding. She said,

"I went in there and told my boss that I wasn't interested in getting in a big fight over this. I wanted us to listen and try to understand one another."

The truth is, her intent was honorable. She was sincerely interested in improving her work as well as the relationship with her boss. As painful as it might be, she knew she needed to better understand where her boss was coming from as well as furthering her boss's understanding of her viewpoint in order to improve the situation. Because she was able to maintain behaviors throughout the meeting that were consistent with her original intent, she was able to influence her boss's behavior. According to my friend, the meeting went surprisingly well. She was genuinely pleased with the results.

What would this conversation have looked like had my friend determined that her desired intent was to "nail the boss"? My bet is that she would have gotten exactly what she planted. Her dishonorable intent would have been communicated to the boss who would have had no desire to participate in a conversation of this nature. The fulfilled intention of "nail the boss" would probably have looked like some variation of an attack and protect interaction between the two parties.

Once again, it's not to say that, with an honorable intent, we've got it made in terms of fundamental conversations. But it does get us pointed in the right direction. I worked with a Department of Veterans Affairs hospital director who felt that it was time for the hospital leadership to regroup and improve their working relationships. Resources were getting tighter, there were increasing demands and requirements from regulatory agencies, morale among staff had dropped, and the rate of change, both organizationally and technologically, was incredible. If they were going to maintain their focus of quality patient care, now more than ever, the executive leadership team and service managers needed to function as a cohesive group. The heartfelt intent of the director was improved teamwork and support for one another. He called together his executive leadership team and service managers to discuss how to enhance their working relationships, in order to work better together.

Keep in mind the context of this meeting. These people were in the midst of getting hammered by a lot of forces beyond their immediate control. They were already working well beyond a fifty-hour week. These are the very circumstances that push people's stress levels into overdrive and encourage anxiety, frustration, mistrust, territorialism, and cynicism among co-workers. In a meeting such as this, you're basically asking people to take time from their already overextended work week to talk about something many of them doubt will have any benefits and, in fact, might only make matters worse.

When the meeting began, all eyes were on the director. Everyone in the room was looking for cues (remember the farmer and the cowboy?) as to his intentions. His opening message was brief. He spoke of his personal commitment to veterans, the difficult times in health care, and his own concern and apprehension as a leader. He voiced his pride in the talent and dedication of the group that was gathered together. He asked others to join him that morning to discuss the nature of their work as leaders in this organization, what was required to do the work, and how they could support each other to accomplish their mission. He felt there was room for improvement, starting with himself. This meeting was an opportunity to dialogue about their working relationships and to explore ways to improve them.

The director had everyone's attention. His original seed intention (improved working relationships) previously planted had now been articulated to the larger group. His sincerity struck a chord of hope and interest with the group. Ever so slowly, the seed began to grow.

For the next couple of hours, people had an opportunity to voice their hopes and concerns. They talked about their shared mission and how there was a heavy leadership burden associated with this mission, including feelings of isolation and an inability to meet both work and home-life demands. By the end of the meeting, there was a greater understanding of just how connected they were to one another and how much teamwork was required to get the job done. For example, when one part of the leadership team made a resource decision, there was a ripple effect for the rest of the group. Many people, because of their own intense work demands and responsibilities, weren't aware of how their resource decisions could impact others.

Overall, the director's intentions set the course for the conversation. Because they were honorable, the group allowed that original seed to sprout. How well this leadership group continues to improve their working relationships with one another depends on their ability to maintain the organizational discipline and concentration to stay with it. In essence, their meeting created an honorable *group* intention, one that holds even more power than any *individual* intention. But as with the corn, it has to be attended to if it's going to mature into something of value.

As we work together, it may take a long time for others to gain a sense of the sincerity and truth of our intentions. That's why it's so important to continue to demonstrate behaviors consistent with our words and to encourage co-worker feedback on how our words and actions are perceived.

Sometimes, intentions must be repeated over a period of time before they are actually heard and acknowledged. Other times, they have to be reframed in a language that is more understandable for a particular audience. There will also be times when our intentions for fundamental conversations are honorable, but the interest of co-workers in participating in them and turning them into a *group* intention, for whatever reason, simply isn't there. When this occurs, we have to accept that our job was merely to plant a seed without expecting the seed to mature in the near future. We can then refocus our influence and intentions to areas where we can make a difference.

● GUIDELINE #3:
MOVE TO A STATE OF ATTENTION

When you're in a state of attention, you're making a conscious choice to focus and keep your attention in the present moment. Concentration, skill, and discipline are required. Similar to driving in a severe rainstorm, if you don't want to have an accident, you have to pay complete attention to your driving and the surrounding conditions. To do this, you have to fully concentrate, call upon your finest driving skills, and have the self-discipline to draw yourself back to the present moment if your mind wanders.

When we're in a state of attention during fundamental conversations, we're more able to communicate effectively. The state of attention supports us in our efforts to avoid raw debate and polite discussion and facilitate skillful discussion and dialogue that were described earlier. This attention allows us to fully engage in the creative and problem-solving processes that are desirable and possible as we make agreements.

To move to this state, we first have to acknowledge that this conversation deserves our attention, which is really no more than a shift in consciousness. As when driving the car in the rainstorm, we consciously choose to focus on the immediate task while detaching from other thoughts. The more we practice this, the better we get at maintaining our concentration.

Second, we need to demonstrate effective communication skills. These skills are what keep us on the road during fundamental conversations, promoting an atmosphere of trust and confidence among co-workers. Just like the car driver, the more skill we have, the more we and other passengers recognize that although the situation is difficult and a bit frightening, we have the ability to do what it takes to arrive safely at our destination.

In fundamental conversations, we're trying to encourage the expression of diverse viewpoints rather than stifle them. At the same time, we're trying to create a common belief (and skills to back it up) that the group has the ability to deal with the diverse viewpoints constructively. Ideally, the group will be as satisfied with the way the conversation was conducted as they are with any agreements reached.

Conducting a conversation using effective communication skills isn't complicated. In most conversations, everyone just wants the opportunity to present their views without interruption, and they want to be heard and understood. Even if other co-workers disagree with us, we don't want to be belittled or de-valued because we expressed ourselves. We want our self-respect and dignity kept intact during the process. The techniques for doing this are not revolutionary but timeless in their substance and potential use.

We may already practice these skills, albeit in an underdeveloped state. If we're going to conduct fundamental conversations in the workplace, each of us must strive to maximize our abilities to listen and talk to one another. We have to learn to use these skills habitually, rather than intermittently.

●THREE COMMUNICATION SKILLS THAT HELP YOU MOVE TO A STATE OF ATTENTION

There are three primary communication skills that help you move to a state of attention: (1) listening for understanding; (2) expressing your thinking clearly; and (3) promoting a constructive atmosphere. There are also some toolkit actions and phrases to help demonstrate those skills. If used with sincerity, and not to manipulate people or situations, they will help improve interactions with co-workers.

Developing and using the communication skills are critical. What you say, how you say it, and the tone you set by your very presence can make an enormous difference in how others experience their interactions with you. Making appropriate use of what's in your toolkit can help you align your communication efforts with your intentions. You need both honorable intentions and skills to communicate effectively.

● SKILL #1:

Listening for Understanding

When you listen for understanding, you are trying to gain clarity about the other person's viewpoint. You're trying to get a picture of his or her thinking. Sometimes this is extraordinarily difficult, like listening to the radio when there's a lot of static. It's hard to hear. But each of you has the power to lower that static, just by watching your own patterns of thinking and feeling, asking questions, and paraphrasing your interpretation of what you heard.

Each of us can be the biggest interference when it comes to listening for understanding. Part of the communication static includes interpretations and assumptions we make about what the other person is thinking or saying. They may or may not be accurate. In addition, we carry our own set of baggage from our past that often includes anxieties, fears, or resentments, some of which have nothing to do with the current conversation. All these things keep us from hearing what is being said to us.

This happened to me when my mother had surgery to have a malignant thyroid removed. Following the surgery, the doctor spoke for several minutes with my father, brother, and me about the results of the surgery, the implications, and recommended follow-up treatment. Our family all asked questions and carefully listened to the doctor's responses. It wasn't until after the doctor left and the three of us huddled before contacting my sister that we realized we had all heard different pieces of the information the doctor had provided. Because of our own anxious states of mind, we were unable to individually capture and absorb everything the doctor was telling us.

A lesson learned is that sometimes it takes a while to understand the message being sent. It's not always captured during one interaction. Sometimes we have to rephrase questions or ask the sender to further describe their intended meaning. And sometimes we have to temporarily suspend our own emotions, attitudes, and thinking. That means we have to consciously set these things aside, as best we can, for a brief time to allow for a static-free environment for hearing the intent of the incoming message. We have to give the speaker our full attention.

Questions to ask yourself as you listen to others:

1. Am I allowing the other person to finish sentences without interruption? Am I checking for understanding by paraphrasing? Is what I heard what the speaker intended?

Toolkit Sample Phrases:

- So what you're saying is . . . ?

- Let me see if I understand. You're telling me that . . . ?

2. Do I ask questions for further understanding in a way that sincerely demonstrates an interest in wanting or needing to know more?

Toolkit Sample Phrases:

- When you use the term . . . what do you mean?

- I'm not sure I understand the part about . . . could you explain that a bit further?

- How do you feel about that?

- Could you tell me how you arrived at that conclusion?

- What data led you to that line of thinking?

- How would your suggestion affect or relate to . . . ?

● SKILL #2:

Expressing Your Thinking Clearly

There are two parts to this skill. First, in fundamental conversations, it's critical to actually verbalize your thoughts to others, rather than expecting them to mind-read where you're coming from. Second, you need to speak clearly, remaining targeted and focused in your presentation of ideas. To do both, it helps to make your thinking process "visible," which means you share out loud what you think or feel and how you arrived at your conclusion.

As we know, we often get into communication trouble when we believe others carry the same assumptions or common meanings for words and situations that we do. When we make our thinking process visible we're reducing the likelihood that this will occur. By using examples or data, we give the listener additional information that enlarges their picture of our perspective.

For example, the doctor used this technique when he spoke with our family after my mother's surgery. He stated how my mother's prognosis for recovery was extremely high because, throughout his years of experience with this type of surgery, almost all his patients had fully recovered. He went on to provide additional national data that supported his statement (and enlarged our picture of his perspective).

We also get into communication trouble when we ramble. Some people believe more is better, so they continue to repeat themselves, hoping that the repetition will clarify their message. Communication is a lot more effective when you make a few simple statements that reflect the essence of your thoughts and then pause to check for understanding of those statements.

Questions to ask yourself as you express your thoughts to others:

1. Do I make a clear statement of my overall perspective, supported by examples and additional data, as appropriate? Do I make my thinking process visible?

Toolkit Sample Phrases:

- Here's what I think/feel and here's how I arrived at that conclusion.

- I would like to see us do...because in my experience . . .

- When I look at the supporting data it leads me to believe . . .

- These are the assumptions that led me to this conclusion.

- I'm not sure where I stand on this issue because . . .

- Here's where I struggle because . . .

2. Do I frequently pause to check for understanding?

Toolkit Sample Phrases:

- Let me pause to ask if there are questions about what I just said?

- What other information could I share with you that would help you further understand what I'm saying?

- What are your thoughts or feelings at this time?

- Would you share with me your interpretation of what I just said?

- What were the key points you heard?

- In what specific areas do you need further clarification?

● **SKILL #3:**

Promoting a Constructive Atmosphere

In conversations, the atmosphere relates to the tone or feel of the interaction. Sometimes the tone is subtle, sometimes it's intense, but it always affects how we experience the conversation, as well as the outcome itself. Most of us know what this is like. For example, we'll leave a meeting where we feel drained or exhausted because of the palpable hostility in the room. Other times, we'll meet with co-workers and feel energized as a result of the conversation.

In fundamental conversations, a constructive atmosphere is one where co-workers focus on solving problems and reaching agreements in a way that stimulates flexible thinking while demonstrating respect for all. Trust is significantly enhanced in a constructive atmosphere. We're more comfortable presenting diverse perspectives or questioning others' thinking because there's a shared belief (with supporting behaviors) that co-workers aren't wed to their egos and positions. When everyone is exploring shared interests, differences of opinion can actually serve to drive the group further toward creative resolutions, and away from satisfying an individual agenda or finding the quick fix. In a constructive atmosphere, it can actually become enjoyable to problem-solve with co-workers. For these reasons, each of us needs to behave in ways that promote this atmosphere.

For example, I was in a meeting where a colleague was presenting an idea. She enthusiastically shared what she wanted to do and why she thought it would provide better customer service. For the next few minutes, we proceeded to grill our co-worker with questions that on the surface were appropriate but in actuality our undertone was filled with negativity. Then a newly hired employee bravely spoke up and said, "You know, I don't think I ever want to bring an idea before this group. All we've done is fire questions at her and tell her how it won't work. We're all so critical. What about offering her encouragement and concrete suggestions?"

I have to admit, I was embarrassed by our group's behavior, as were many of my colleagues. Our original intent for having the meeting was to share ideas and projects, and here we were setting a tone of negativity. In fairness, we were probably all feeling overwhelmed with our own workloads and it carried over into this meeting. And that's an important point to remember. This kind of thing can easily happen unless we maintain our awareness that feelings, behaviors, and language set the tone of the meeting, which in turn, influences the outcome. In this case, our group was willing and able to self-correct, adjusting our behaviors in such a way that they were more closely aligned with our intent of sharing.

As you engage in fundamental conversations, you have a responsibility to promote a constructive atmosphere. You don't have to like everyone you work with (although that enhances your work experience), but you do have to acknowledge that part of your job is to work cooperatively with one another, respect others' rights to their viewpoints, and actively seek common ground for working productively together.

So how do you create this constructive atmosphere during your fundamental conversations? As with the other guidelines and skills, you work from the inside-out, looking at your own thoughts and behaviors first. To help do this, think of times when you demonstrated the utmost respect for another person, even (and especially) when you disagreed with their viewpoint. How did you act? What was your tone during the conversation? How did you express yourself and still emit a feeling of cooperation and continued openness? Or, what about the times you've marveled as you've seen others maintain their composure, and even what you might call majesty, as they've dealt with difficult situations or people who had no interest in maintaining a constructive atmosphere. How did they act to maintain such a presence? What did they do or say to help the group refocus on their mutual task? What impact did it have on the group and outcome?

Questions to ask yourself as you strive to promote a constructive atmosphere:

1. Am I aware of and do I assume responsibility for my own biases, feelings, and ego needs during conversations? Am I able to temporarily suspend them in order to be fully present in the immediate conversation?

2. Do I use appropriate verbal language and body language (such as eye contact and an open and relaxed stance) to encourage and support a constructive atmosphere?

3. Am I aware of my breathing so that if things get tense, I can consciously slow my breathing until it is relaxed and even?

Toolkit Sample Phrases:

- Thanks for sharing that information.

- Each of us has our own unique perspective of this issue. Before we jump to any resolution, let's use our collective understanding and knowledge to gain an overall picture of the situation.

- Please let me offer another way of looking at this issue.

- Let's pause and make sure we've heard and understood everyone's perspective.

- [Person's name], you're on the front lines of this thing, what do you think?

- How might we build on the ideas we've talked about here today?

- Thanks for your ideas. They were helpful because . . .

- We've got some areas of disagreement. Let's go through each of these areas and see if we can systematically begin to sort this thing out.

4. When the group gets stuck, do I help the group move on while maintaining the focus?

Toolkit Sample Phrases:

- We seem to be at an impasse here. What can we do to help ourselves move forward?

- It feels like we're stuck. How can we build off our common interests and create something that makes sense?

- What if we were to . . . ?

- What else could we consider to look at this situation differently?

- What other options might we consider?

- We've done some solid work so far. Let's see if we can push ourselves a little further.

- What have we done before to help ourselves move forward?

- How about giving ourselves a few minutes of down time to rethink this individually before we try to collectively go any further?

There's a final caution to keep in mind as you use the tools to develop your communication skills. You don't want or need a bunch of communication parrots in your workplace programmed to say a specific phrase at a particular time. That would not only be artificial, it would also deny individuals' abilities to contribute to fundamental conversations. Some people are innately funny, others creative or insightful, and still others offer the ability to put things in concrete terms. When you put all these people and qualities together in the same room using the communication tools, each with their own unique spin, there's an authenticity, richness, and spontaneity that emerge. Therefore, you need to experiment with the tools in your individual toolkit, practicing what phrases or behaviors resonate with your own personal style and which ones seem artificial. Comparing your perceptions with a trusted colleague who can tell you how others react to your words and actions and in what ways the group process is impacted is often helpful.

Once again, sincerity and honorable intentions count a great deal. You're striving for improvement, not perfection. So you do what you can, knowing that if each individual concentrates on improving his or her own ability to move to a state of attention, the group's overall capacity to conduct meaningful conversations will be greatly enhanced.

● GUIDELINE #4:
KEEP AT IT TO KEEP IT GOING

For fundamental conversations to really impact how we collectively work together, we have to complete the entire conversation cycle. This means honoring our agreements with follow-through behaviors and actions as well as maintaining constant feedback among co-workers as to, "How are we doing?" and "How do we make this better?" We're trying to align our thoughts, actions, and resources with the stated agreements at every possible opportunity. We have to *keep at it to keep it going*, so that eventually it becomes a way of life in our workplace.

Fundamental conversations should be viewed as a way of conducting our work, rather than as sporadic interactions with co-workers. It's really a work-style choice, not all that different than a commitment to living a healthy lifestyle. When you commit to a healthy lifestyle, you create a mindset for that lifestyle and then continually align your behaviors and resources in ways that are compatible with that mindset.

Living a healthy lifestyle requires long-term changes in your behavior as well as a redistribution of such resources as time, energy, and money. You can't expect to occasionally exercise or eat right and think you're going to have a major impact on your health. At first, it may feel strange or forced to buy and eat the proper food, make time for exercise, and get the proper amount of rest, but as time progresses these behaviors become so habitual and natural that you can't imagine being any other way. You're unable to separate the concept of "healthy lifestyle" from who you are and how you live your daily life.

Ideally, we make this lifestyle choice at a point when our health is still relatively good. We make the shift because we know it's the right thing to do. Not only can it lengthen our lives, it significantly impacts the quality of how we live our lives. Sometimes our choice for a healthy lifestyle is made for us, such as when our bodies can no longer sustain a particular long-term unhealthy habit, thus forcing us to re-evaluate and make adjustments to our behaviors.

In using fundamental conversations, we are striving to do something similar. We are choosing to create a healthier way to conduct our work by regularly talking and reaching agreements with one another about issues of mutual importance. As we do this, we continually strive to align our behaviors and resources so that they are consistent with that choice. We come to recognize that fundamental conversations aren't separate from our work. Rather, they are an integral part of how we relate to others in the workplace. The trigger questions are merely tools to help us think, talk, and act in ways that promote a systems approach and help us work as one. Ideally, workgroups are eventually able to reach a point where collectively they can't imagine another way of doing business.

There's a popular saying, "pay me now, or pay me later," and it applies to the use of fundamental conversations in the workplace. One way or another we have to "pay up" by doing what it takes to work cooperatively with co-workers. It's just a matter of when. We know that fundamental conversations, just like the healthy lifestyle, can promote a state of wellness in the workplace and yet many of us continue to demonstrate old habits that are often highly destructive. As individuals and workgroups, we can either commit to making changes now, while we still have some semblance of good health and are able to fully participate in creating a constructive approach to our work, or we can wait until we're so weakened by ongoing dissent and tension that it's far more difficult to reverse the damage.

When we come to view fundamental conversations as a way of life, there are a variety of strategies to keep at it to keep it going, individually as well as organizationally. As with every other suggested guideline, we use an inside-out approach. First, we assume responsibility for our own thoughts, actions, and behaviors. Then, we work with others to create structures and processes to support the entire workgroup in their collective feedback and improvement efforts.

There was a health care executive that a colleague and I interviewed as part of a national study to identify the best practices of leaders whose VA medical centers successfully implemented total quality improvement. The executive's hospital was recognized as being in the forefront of the continuous improvement movement.

What struck us during the interview was this man's absolute, total, and deeply spiritual commitment to improving the quality of care for veterans in an environment that simultaneously recognized and valued the hospital staff. He shared with us his initial doubts and anxieties about making continuous improvement a way of life (rather than sporadic occurrences) for both himself and all employees. He felt it was the right thing to do but he also realized that this was a different way of doing business; one that would require all employees, first and foremost himself, to think and act differently. He described how over a period of months, numerous employees engaged in a series of improvement conversations where agreements were reached. Then came the greatest challenge of all—how to keep at it so that the cycle of improvement could continue. How were they going to keep their agreements in the forefront of their thinking and actions on a daily basis?

The executive told his us he became relentless in his efforts. He worked hard to "walk the talk" making sure he didn't ask others to do anything he wasn't willing to do himself. He also shared how he used every opportunity (in meetings, hospital employee forums, informal conversations with staff, community speaking engagements) to share the message of continuous improvement, even to the point of being repetitious.

Each time a staff request was made to allocate resources (whether it was time, people, money, space, equipment, etc.) questions were raised such as, "How does this request fit in with our previous agreements? Is it consistent? Are we actually putting our money where our mouths are?" For example, if there wasn't an alignment between the proposed resource request and the medical center mission, vision, core values, customer requirements, and strategic plan, then the resource request was nixed. When there was alignment, the leadership team made sure that everyone was told why the resource request was approved and how it fit into the overall agreements that had been previously determined.

These were effective strategies. All staff were continually flooded, in a variety of ways, with consistent messages that served to remind them not only of their commitment to participate in continuous improvement, but also what that commitment meant in terms of expected behaviors with patients and one another on a daily basis. The leadership regularly acknowledged, thanked, and rewarded staff who modeled these desirable behaviors. Eventually, this way of life became more pervasive throughout the entire organization, with staff from all levels recognizing the importance of linking conversational agreements to thoughts, behaviors, and resource allocation.

During this same study, there was another interesting discovery. The leaders most able to spread continuous improvement throughout their organizations used mistakes as opportunities for learning. Therefore, when things didn't work out as well as originally planned or when there was an error in judgment by an individual or group, the approach was not to belittle, ridicule, or punish. Rather, it was to ask, "What did we learn from this? The next time around, how can we do it better?" Mistakes were viewed as breakdowns in the system and efforts were focused on looking for ways to improve that system. As a result, individual and group learning became a strategy to remind everyone about their original agreements and to make necessary adjustments to those agreements as needed. Equally important, the doors to creativity and innovation within the organization were also opened.

This example demonstrates seven specific strategies to help workgroups using fundamental conversations to keep at it to keep it going:

1. Make a personal commitment to honor agreements.

2. Walk the talk. Honor the agreements by acting in ways that are consistent with the agreements.

3. Jointly discuss among co-workers potential barriers that could keep people from honoring commitments and identify strategies to reduce those barriers.

4. Use every opportunity (meetings, one-on-one conversations, public forums, etc.) to discuss, promote, or remind co-workers how behaviors and actions relate to the fundamental conversations and agreements. For example, during a one-on-one conversation with a co-worker about a mutual project, you might briefly review any agreements about the overall goal of the project and who is doing what to achieve that goal. Further conversations would involve checking in with one another as to how well those agreements were being followed and if adjustments needed to be made. Or, it may be a situation where a coach is sharing with community members how the focus and actions of the coaching staff are related to the vision for the overall program and the needs of the team members.

The coach is trying to remind folks that, "This is what we're about and this is how our actions relate to what we're about," which is key to getting everyone moving in one direction— coaches, parents, and the community.

5. Align all resource decisions with fundamental conversations and agreements. Before allocating resources, ask, "Is this distribution of resources consistent with our agreements?" If it isn't consistent, make a conscious choice to either deny the resource allocation, or review and adjust the previous agreements. For example, if an organization has determined

that improving customer service is a major priority, then resources should be aligned to support that priority. To divert needed resources for someone's pet project doesn't make sense. If, however, there's a sudden and immediate need for building repairs, funds and human resources intended for improving customer service may in fact need to be redirected toward the repair effort. What's important is the awareness among co-workers as to the need for the shift and the recognition of how that shift may impact their work.

6. De-personalize mistakes or glitches. Use them as opportunities for individual and group learning, and remember that it's unrealistic to think everything will run smoothly all the time. Ask, "What have we learned? How can we do this better? Where did the breakdown occur?"

7. Acknowledge, thank, and/or reward co-workers for honoring agreements. Seek co-workers' input for how to do even better.

Fundamental conversations are meant to be dynamic. We have to do our part (and encourage others to do likewise) to keep at it in order to keep it going. As part of this ongoing process, the conversations take on a life of their own, often evolving into something far greater than the original conversation.

Conclusion

The concepts in this book are not new. Rather, it is their fundamental nature that makes them so worthy of our attention. The conversations, cycle, and guidelines given here are based on universal principles that promote our ability to work with one another. These principles are steeped in centuries of human experience, wisdom, and growth. The book content merely repackages those principles and experiences in such a way as to draw attention to our interdependence and connectedness with one another in today's workplace. Hopefully, readers will gain a common sense and practical framework to think, talk, and act in ways that foster healthy conversations.

All of us are a part of an incredible human experience. Who we are and how we conduct ourselves in our workplaces represent an aspect of our individual and collective journey toward learning and growth. Within the context of our work lives we have many opportunities to express our unique abilities, skills, and qualities. We also have opportunities to recognize, develop, and honor others' talents. However time consuming, difficult, or painful, it is in the process of sharing these riches that the potential for genuine understanding and cooperation exists among co-workers.

We certainly *do* have much to talk about in our workplaces. Fundamental conversations are the tools to get us talking about the right things in the right way. Our own awareness, commitment, and skills are what open the door to the possibilities of new ways of thinking and working together as one. It is then that the cooperative journeys in our workplaces can truly begin.

About the Author

Christine Williams, PhD, facilitates, speaks, and consults with organizations throughout the United States to help people talk with one another in constructive and productive ways. She has worked "in the trenches" for over twenty years with health care, educational, manufacturing, and nonprofit organizations—particularly in the areas of continuous improvement, communication, and strategic planning.

With her extensive experience in leadership development, Chris has worked with hundreds of health care executives and managers. From 1989–1996, she codeveloped and served as the project manager of a cutting-edge national executive development program for clinical leaders from the Veterans Health Administration, Department of Veterans Affairs. These three-week leadership programs were specifically designed for physicians and other health care clinicians transitioning into the role of clinical executives.

Chris has a doctorate in higher education, a master's degree in guidance and counseling, and a bachelor's degree in education. In 1992, Chris founded Focus Consulting Group, a firm established to help groups improve their capacity and skills to work collaboratively.

Chris lives in Bath, Ohio, and can be contacted at www.focusconsultgroup.com.